the Leopard Gecko Manual

2nd Edition

Philippe de Vosjoli
with Thomas Mazorlig,
Roger Klingenberg, DVM,
Ron Tremper, and Brian Viets, PhD

THE LEOPARD GECKO MANUAL

CompanionHouse Books™ is an imprint of Fox Chapel Publishing.

Project Team
Editorial Director: Kerry Bogert
Editor: Amy Deputato
Copy Editor: Laura Taylor
Design: Wendy Reynolds
Index: Jay Kreider

ISBN 978-1-62008-259-1

Library of Congress Cataloging-in-Publication Data

Names: De Vosjoli, Philippe, author. | Mazorlig, Tom, author. | Klingenberg,
    Roger J., 1954- author. | Tremper, Ron, author. | Viets, Brian E., author.
Title: The leopard gecko manual : expert advice for keeping and caring for a
    healthy leopard gecko / Philippe de Vosjoli, Tom Mazorlig, Robert
    Klingenberg, DVM, Ron Tremper, and Brian Viets, PhD.
Description: 2nd edition. | Mount Joy, PA : Fox Chapel Publishing, [2017] |
    Includes bibliographical references and index.
Identifiers: LCCN 2017027304 (print) | LCCN 2017027735 (ebook) | ISBN
    9781620082256 (ebook) | ISBN 9781620082591 (softcover)
Subjects: LCSH: Leopard geckos as pets—Handbooks, manuals, etc.
Classification: LCC SF459.G35 (ebook) | LCC SF459.G35 D42 2017 (print) | DDC
    639.3/95—dc23
LC record available at https://lccn.loc.gov/2017027304

This book has been published with the intent to provide accurate and authoritative information in regard to the subject matter within. While every precaution has been taken in the preparation of this book, the author and publisher expressly disclaim any responsibility for any errors, omissions, or adverse effects arising from the use or application of the information contained herein. The techniques and suggestions are used at the reader's discretion and are not to be considered a substitute for veterinary care. If you suspect a medical problem, consult your veterinarian.

Fox Chapel Publishing
903 Square Street
Mount Joy, PA 17552

www.facebook.com/companionhousebooks

We are always looking for talented authors. To submit an idea, please send a brief inquiry to acquisitions@foxchapelpublishing.com.

Printed and bound in China
24 23 22   6 8 10 9 7 5

CONTENTS

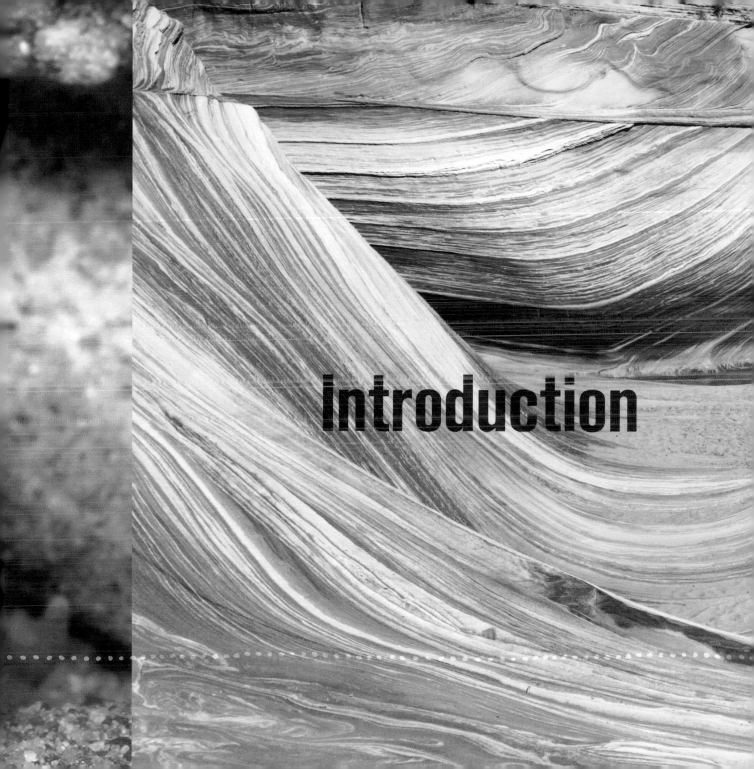

Introduction

S ince the publication of my first book on leopard geckos in 1990, the herpetoculture of this species has undergone a revolution, transforming the leopard gecko into the first domesticated species of lizard. The leopard gecko is now the reptilian version of the parakeet or goldfish. As with goldfish, selective breeding for xanthism (predominance of yellow and orange skin pigments produced by cells called *xanthophores*) launched the course for domestication. Today, a number of leopard gecko morphs are commercially available, with many more on the horizon. As with fancy goldfish or koi carp, breeders eagerly seek prize specimens, which can fetch hundreds or even thousands of dollars.

Like other domesticated animals, the leopard gecko has certain characteristics that make it particularly suitable for this kind of endeavor. It is one of the hardiest of all lizard species: easy to keep, easy to breed, and potentially long-lived. It is a convenient size, neither too small to be appreciated and handled nor so large that it presents risks or requires an enclosure that can't be readily integrated into the average household. And the leopard gecko is undeniably beautiful, from the near-velvet texture of its skin to its gold eyes and pastel shades of color. Like other animals developed as forms of living art, the leopard gecko is extremely variable in color and pattern. These lizards also have nice personalities, by reptilian standards. By the time they are adults, many leopard geckos become quite docile and are slow and deliberate in their movements. The leopard gecko is one of the finest pets you could own.

CHAPTER 1

INTRODUCING THE LEOPARD GECKO

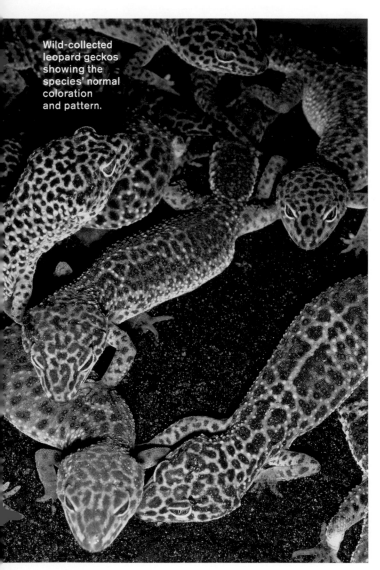

Wild-collected leopard geckos showing the species' normal coloration and pattern.

To start with the very basics, what is a leopard gecko? Leopard geckos are small lizards that are members of a hugely diverse group called *geckos*. Normally colored leopard geckos are pale yellow with numerous darker spots, which is why they are called *leopard* geckos. They are personable, with ever-smiling faces that have won them legions of fans. They are most active at night and feed primarily on insects and any other small animals that they can catch. Their attractive appearance and ease of care have made these lizards one of the most popular pet reptiles in the world.

Scientifically speaking, all geckos belong to an infraorder called Gekkota and are classified into seven different families. Older references consider the geckos to all belong to one family, Geckonidae, but Geckonidae is now considered as just one of the families of geckos within the infraorder Gekkota. Geckos are believed to be more closely related to each other than to other lizards. There are at least 1,500 species of geckos found in warm regions around the globe.

With a group as large and diverse as the geckos, they do not share many features in common, but one thing that nearly all geckos do is vocalize. Geckos can call, chirp, or bark, depending on the species. Their calls announce their presence to other geckos as a way of establishing territory. Some geckos use them as a threat, and most geckos will

Why Use Scientific Names?

If you are new to keeping reptiles as pets, it may seem odd to see scientific names (these are the strange-looking words in italics that come after the familiar name of an animal). Scientific names are used commonly within the reptile- and fish-keeping communities.

The scientific name of an animal is agreed upon by the global scientific community and is used instead of any regional names for a given animal. The leopard gecko is *Eublepharis macularius* whether you are in Maine or Mozambique, whether you are speaking English or Estonian.

Scientific names ensure that everyone is discussing the same organism. If someone says "green tree frog," you don't know if that person means the commonly seen green tree frog of the United States or another type of tree frog that happens to be green. However, if the person instead refers to *Hyla cinerea*, you can be sure that it is the common American frog known as the green tree frog.

Scientific names are composed of two words. The first word is capitalized and is called the *generic* name. A genus is a group of closely related species, and this word tells you which genus the animal is in. Leopard geckos are in the genus *Eublepharis*. The second word is always lowercase and is called the *specific* name. This word tells you the exact species in question. For the leopard gecko, this is *macularius*. When you put the two together, it forms a unique combination that identifies the exact species.

On occasion, you may see a scientific name that has three parts. The third word is the subspecies. A subspecies is a variation of a species. The variation is not great enough for these animals to be considered a separate species, but it is distinct enough to be given some recognition. With further research, sometimes subspecies are elevated to full species; other times, the subspecies designation is eliminated because the variation was not considered truly distinct.

When a scientific name is used once in a given work, the generic name can be abbreviated to the first letter when it appears again: for example, *E. macularius*. With subspecies, you can abbreviate both the generic and specific names and retain the full subspecies name.

make a lot of noise when restrained or surprised. In fact, the word *gecko* derives from the noises made by the Tokay gecko, an especially common and noisy gecko of India and Southeast Asia. Leopard geckos are quiet for the most part, but they will bark or squeal when they feel threatened. They may also emit a squeaky hiss when startled.

FAMILY MATTERS

Leopard geckos belong to the family Eublepharidae, which includes all geckos with movable eyelids. All other geckos lack eyelids; instead, they have clear scales covering their eyes, which they clean off with their tongues. The eyelids of leopard geckos lend them a lot of their cute charm.

The members of the family Eublepharidae also lack toe pads—more properly called *subdigital setae*—pads of tiny,

hairlike, scaly projections on the undersides of the toes. These toe pads give the other geckos their famous climbing abilities. Therefore, leopard geckos and other eublepharid geckos are not able to climb smooth, vertical surfaces.

The family Eublepharidae is divided in two subfamilies: Eublepharinae and Aeluroscalabotinae. The subfamily Eublepharinae includes all geckos with eyelids except one: the odd little Indonesian

Leopard geckos' feet lack toe pads, rendering them unable to climb smooth surfaces.

creature known as the cat gecko, *Aeluroscalabotes felinus*. The cat gecko is classified in its own separate subfamily, Aeluroscalabotinae. The rare cat gecko is found in parts of Indonesia and Southeast Asia and is maintained and bred by only a small number of dedicated hobbyists. Some of the other well-known eublepharids (geckos with eyelids) in herpetoculture include the banded geckos (*Coleonyx* sp.) of the Western Hemisphere, the cave geckos (*Goniurosaurus* sp.) of East Asia, the African fat-tailed geckos (*Hemitheconyx caudicinctus*), and the occasionally imported African clawed gecko (*Holodactylus africanus*).

This book focuses on the popular leopard gecko but includes information on keeping and breeding all of the eublepharids found in the herp hobby. All members of the genus *Eublepharis* are known as leopard geckos. Besides the common leopard gecko, *Eublepharis macularius* of the pet trade, there are the Turkmenian leopard gecko, *E. turcmenicus*; the East Indian leopard gecko, *E. hardwickii*; the Iraqi or Iranian leopard gecko, *E. angramainyu*; and the West Indian leopard gecko, *E. fuscus*. The latter is of particular interest to hobbyists. It was initially described as a subspecies of the common leopard gecko (*E. macularius fuscus*) (Borner 1981) and then later elevated to full species status (Das 1997). The West Indian leopard gecko is one of the largest geckos, with a snout–vent length of nearly 10 inches.

Leopard Gecko Taxonomy

Kingdom: Animalia
Phylum: Chordata
Class: Reptilia
Order: Squamata
Infraorder: Gekkota
Family: Eublepharidae
Genus: *Eublepharis*
Species: *macularius*

The other leopard geckos are exceedingly rare in captivity. Most reptile keepers will never see one outside of a zoo, with the possible exception of the Iranian leopard gecko, which has been imported in small numbers. Because they are wild-caught, rare in the pet trade, and expensive, they are best left to advanced keepers and breeders.

THE BASICS

The leopard gecko is found in Afghanistan, northwestern India, and Pakistan. Its habitat is desert and dry grasslands. The majority of the early captive stock was imported from Pakistan, although some imports

The leopard gecko's natural habitats include deserts and dry grasslands.

are said to have originated in Afghanistan. Nearly all of the leopard geckos for sale nowadays have been hatched from eggs laid in captivity.

SIZE AND GROWTH

Adult leopard geckos can attain a maximum length of a little more than 8 inches (20.5 cm). Hatchlings have a total length of 3.25 to 3.5 inches (around 9 cm). Giant leopard geckos have been selectively bred over generations to reach a larger size. Giant leopard geckos can reach about a foot (30.5 cm) in length and a weight of 6 ounces (170 grams).

Compared to large lizards, the relative growth rate of leopard geckos is minimal, a twentyfold increase in weight from hatchling to adult. Hatchlings weigh about .10 of an ounce (2.5 to 3 grams). Adults typically weigh from 1.5 to a little more than 2 ounces (45 to 60 grams) but can attain a weight of 3.5 ounces (100 grams). Young adults can breed at 1 to 1.2 ounces (30 to 35 grams), and they usually reach adult size by around eighteen months.

LONGEVITY

Leopard geckos are long-lived lizards. There is record of a male that was more than twenty-eight years old at the St. Louis Zoo. Herpetoculturist Ron Tremper reported another captive male specimen that lived to almost thirty-two years of age. Female leopard geckos generally have shorter life spans than males. The longevity record for a female leopard gecko is twenty years and ten months (Slavens and Slavens 1997). The normal life span of a pet leopard gecko is up to ten years, although males can live up to twenty years.

SEXING

Males are somewhat more heavy-bodied and have slightly broader heads and thicker necks than females. The only reliable method for determining sex is to look at the underside of the animal. A male has a V-shaped row of enlarged preanal pores in front of the vent (the combined opening for wastes and mating) that may exude a waxy secretion. Another obvious characteristic of a mature male is the presence of paired swellings at the base of the tail. These swellings are called the *hemipenal bulges* because they house the hemipenes, which are the male sexual organs in lizards and snakes. In contrast, females have preanal pits rather than enlarged pores and lack paired swellings at the base of the tail.

Close-up of a male leopard gecko's tail base, showing enlarged preanal pores and hemipenal bulges.

Close-up of a female leopard gecko's tail base.

Juveniles that are at least one month old can be sexed with some reliability by checking for developing preanal pores (in contrast to the barely hinted pits of female hatchlings). To look for these on juveniles, you will likely need a magnifying glass.

You might think that if you never intend to breed your leopard gecko, it doesn't matter whether you have a male or a female or that you don't need to determine the sex of your pet. However, it can matter for several reasons. For example, male leopard geckos are territorial and often will fight when kept together. If you plan on keeping more than one gecko, you must house only one male per enclosure. A female leopard gecko can sometimes develop eggs even if no male is present. The eggs will be infertile, but you will need to provide her a place to lay them just the same. And pet owners like to know whether their leopard geckos are males or females for naming purposes.

Useful Terms

Every hobby has its own jargon, and keeping reptiles is no exception. Here are some reptile-specific terms you will find in this book.

captive-bred: hatched from an egg that was laid in captivity.

herp: collective term for both reptiles and amphibians.

herper: a person who is interested in herps and has herps as pets; also called a *herp hobbyist* or *herp keeper*.

herpetoculture: the keeping and breeding of herps as pets.

herpetoculturist: someone who practices herpetoculture.

herpetologist: a scientist who studies reptiles and amphibians

snout-vent length (SVL): the length of an animal from the tip of the nose to the vent; in other words, the length of the animal, not including the tail.

vivarium: an enclosure housing reptiles, amphibians, or other small animals, usually containing live plants, soil, and other natural features.

wild-caught: brought into the pet trade from its natural habitat.

CHAPTER 2

YOUR PET LEOPARD GECKO

I f you are reading this book, you are likely already interested in keeping a leopard gecko as a pet. You have already been charmed by the leopard gecko's bright colors and cute face that seems to be perpetually smiling.

If so, you are in great company. Leopard geckos are one of most popular of all reptile pets. They have earned their popularity by being hardy and easy to care for as well as by being docile and having beautiful coloration. Additionally, they are not noisy and—as long as you clean the cage—do not smell. They will even tolerate some handling. If you think you ever want to breed reptiles, leopard geckos are ideal as your first breeding project.

In order to successfully keep a leopard gecko, you need to know where to find leopard geckos, how to pick out a healthy one, and how to handle one safely.

Many adult leopard geckos, especially males, will remain calm with regular but brief periods of handling.

LEOPARD GECKO SOURCES

Leopard geckos are popular pets, but if you've never kept a reptile before, you might not know where to find one. The obvious source is a pet store, and, indeed, that can be a great place to get a leopard gecko. There are also some other options that you might want to consider.

PET STORES

Local and large chain pet-supply stores frequently offer leopard geckos and other small reptiles for sale. Before buying your pet from any store, make sure it's a reputable place. It should be clean and well lit, and not have an offensive odor (within reason—when dealing with live animals, it's nearly impossible to be odor free). All of the animals should be kept in clean conditions appropriate for their species. If the store does not meet these standards, don't reward them with your business.

It is a sound idea to browse the store to see if it carries all the supplies you will need going forward. You will need a source for your food, vitamins, substrate, and more. You may want to see if the store can special-order the particular items or brands you want.

Before buying your gecko, inquire about the store's animal guarantee and return policy. Most stores will guarantee their animals for two days to two weeks. Make sure you understand the store's policy—get it in writing if you can—so that if you end up with an unhealthy gecko or have some other issue, you will have some recourse.

REPTILE SHOWS

In many areas of the United States, there are semi-regular reptile shows, also called reptile expos. These are one- or two-day events that bring together many vendors selling live reptiles, supplies,

Cage before Lizard

Always buy the enclosure and other accessories before you bring a leopard gecko home. Set everything up at least a day in advance and make sure all of the equipment works. Check that the enclosure's temperature falls in the correct range. Arrange the landscape to find the look you want.

Having the vivarium ready before you bring your new pet home lowers the stress it will experience. As soon as you get your gecko home, you can introduce it to its new digs instead of making it wait in a box while you scramble to set up its enclosure.

The leopard gecko's distinct looks and behavioral qualities make it a popular reptile pet.

and related items. One of these shows can be a great source for your leopard gecko. You can find out about reptile shows online or in reptile publications.

At a show, you will likely have many geckos to choose from, and you will be able to see them all up close—but don't just buy the first nice gecko you see. Visit several vendors and be sure to make note of the vendors who have geckos that catch your eye.

Because reptile shows attract both big-name and hobbyist breeders, it can be easier to find specific color varieties—usually called *morphs*—at shows than in pet stores. Shows can also offer good opportunities to talk directly to breeders or other experts about gecko care. Remember to be considerate. While most will perfectly happy to talk to you, they are there to sell animals and supplies. For some, reptile shows may be a significant part of their income. If a vendor you'd really like to talk to is busy with customers, ask for his or her contact information and reach out at another time.

Some of the same rules for buying a gecko at a pet store apply here. Make sure you are getting a healthy gecko. Ask to hold the gecko in which you are interested to get a closer look. If you see someone selling dirty, underweight, or otherwise unhealthy animals at his or her table, choose a different vendor.

Some vendors will offer a guarantee at the show; others will not. It's not necessarily a sign of a bad vendor if he or she won't offer a guarantee. After all, how does the vendor know that you didn't leave the gecko in your hot car for a few hours while you went for lunch? If your chosen vendor does offer a guarantee, be sure that you understand the details and get his or her contact information before you complete the sale.

ONLINE SELLERS

It's becoming more and more common to buy reptiles and other animals via the Internet. Usually this means buying directly from a breeder's website, but you could be buying from a retailer who did not produce the geckos him- or herself.

Leopard gecko lines developed by David Nieves: tangerine (top) and high-contrast with orange tint (bottom).

Buying online might be the best method of obtaining a leopard gecko if you want a specific morph or want to purchase from a specific breeder. Most breeders have photos of their stock on their website. You can select the exact gecko you want and pay via credit card, and the seller will ship the gecko to your door.

The downside of buying online is that you cannot inspect the gecko for health, nor can you check out the breeding facility. It's a good idea to research the vendor's online reputation and avoid those sellers who have many negative reviews. Again, be sure you understand whatever guarantee the seller offers. Most online vendors guarantee only live arrival; that is, they guarantee that the gecko will be alive when it reaches you, but you are on your own afterward.

RESCUES AND SHELTERS

The leopard gecko's popularity means that sometimes geckos are purchased by owners who decide that they no longer want their geckos. These geckos may end up in animal shelters or reptile rescues. If you don't mind starting with an older leopard gecko, or you like the idea of giving an animal a chance at a better life, consider adopting from a shelter or rescue. The best way to find leopard geckos in need of adoption is to go to Petfinder.com, which will direct you to the closest sources of adoptable leopard geckos.

SELECTING A LEOPARD GECKO

Most of the leopard geckos sold in the trade are captive-bred juveniles. Subadults (those of nearly adult size but not yet able to breed), retired breeders, and imports are sporadically available.

WILD IMPORTS VERSUS CAPTIVE BRED

Relatively few wild-collected leopard geckos are now imported into the United States, and they are primarily of interest only to breeders who want to diversify their gene pools. Compared to the captive-bred leopard geckos offered in the pet trade, wild imports typically appear dull-colored, beat up, and thin. Captive-bred and captive-raised animals are best for aspiring leopard gecko owners because they are generally more attractive and healthier than wild forms. Captive-bred geckos are already adapted to living in captivity, so they will not be overly stressed by the move to their new owners' homes. Given the huge numbers of captive-bred leopard geckos available and their advantages over wild-caught ones, there is no

All interactions between children and leopard geckos must be supervised.

reason for anyone other than large-scale breeders to purchase wild-caught leopard geckos.

SIZE

If your interest is captive breeding or having a long-lived pet, then the best choice is an immature leopard gecko less than 6 inches long. You can reliably assume that a gecko of this size is younger than one year old. For beginners, animals at least 4 inches long are better choices than small hatchlings, which tend to be more delicate.

If you are attracted to a particularly large and robust adult, probably a retired breeder, remember that it may be old and, in the case of a female, probably not capable of producing many more eggs. This does not mean that an older gecko will not make an excellent and long-lived pet. The mother of one of the authors adopted a leopard gecko when it was estimated to be five years old, and that lizard was still going strong at the age of twenty-three.

A lavender and yellow leopard gecko.

SEX

Male and female leopard geckos make equally nice pets. If you plan to breed leopard geckos, you will need only one male for every ten or so females, and males cannot be housed together when mature. If you want to introduce a new mutation, such as albinism, into your colony, a single male is a better investment than a single female. If your goal is to beat existing longevity records for the species, a male is also a better choice.

MORPHS

There are many varieties of leopard gecko, and every year seems to bring some new variation. The primary criterion for selecting a morph should be the aesthetic appeal it has for you. If your interest is primarily in the financial benefits of breeding one morph or another, research your market carefully before investing.

The jungle morph is characterized by an irregular dorsal pattern and an unringed tail.

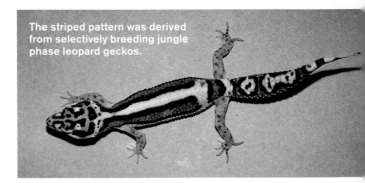
The striped pattern was derived from selectively breeding jungle phase leopard geckos.

HEALTH CONSIDERATIONS

The following guidelines will help you select a potentially healthy leopard gecko. However, careful examination prior to purchase does not always guarantee good health. Diagnosis of illness may also require veterinary examination and testing, such as fecal exams. On two occasions, one of the authors bought what appeared to be relatively healthy animals that were later diagnosed with coccidiosis (a parasitic infestation). On the bright side, most of the captive-bred leopard geckos sold in the pet trade are healthy.

1. The body outline should be smooth, the outline of the hip bones not visible, and the tail rounded without wrinkles that give it a shrunken appearance. In the case of imports, a wrinkled tail may simply mean that a leopard gecko has not been fed for an extended period of time.

2. The mouth, when closed, should appear even, with no jutting upper or lower jaw.

3. Examine the digits (fingers and toes). They should appear even without swelling. No toes should be missing.

4. The eyes should be equal in size. Avoid leopard geckos with small eyes or with large, protruding eyes.

5. If fecal matter is present in the enclosure, examine it for consistency. The feces of healthy leopard geckos are semi-formed and somewhat pellet-like in shape. They are dark with some whitish urates

Don't Buy a Sick Gecko

If you ever see a sick, injured, or otherwise debilitated leopard gecko for sale, you may be tempted to buy it so you can nurse it back to health, but this is a bad idea. Once a reptile is sick enough to show symptoms, it's already very sick and it's likely already too far gone to save it. In trying to save it, you will likely have to expend a significant amount of money and time—to say nothing of the emotional investment. Buying a sick gecko in hopes of saving it is the road to heartbreak. Only experts in the care and rehabilitation of reptiles should attempt to rescue sick geckos.

Another thing to consider is that by paying for a sick animal, you are rewarding the seller for not caring for his or her livestock. If vendors can sell sick animals as well as healthy ones, they have that much less incentive to use their resources for keeping their animals healthy. You may actually encourage the cruel behavior.

As hard as it is to turn your back on a suffering animal, buying a sick gecko is not the way to help. It is best to politely inform the seller that the animal is sick and hope that they respond appropriately. If they do not, take your business elsewhere and inform the seller why you are doing so.

(urine in solid form). Pale, light-colored, or yellow-orange feces; patty-shaped pasty feces; and runny feces are all signs of possible disease.

6. Ask the seller to let you see your chosen leopard gecko up close. It should appear bright-eyed and alert when in your hand. Look at the belly area of the leopard gecko; the vent area should appear flush and clean without swelling, fecal smearing, or caked material.

HOW MANY?

Leopard geckos, like many reptiles, do not require the company of cagemates to fare well. A single animal will thrive when kept by itself. If you want more than one leopard gecko, remember that adult males cannot be kept together or they will fight. Most of the animals sold in the pet trade are females, which can safely be kept together. If you want to breed leopard geckos, it is best to keep one male with several females. As a general rule, animals kept singly tend to maintain more weight and be more brightly colored than those kept in groups.

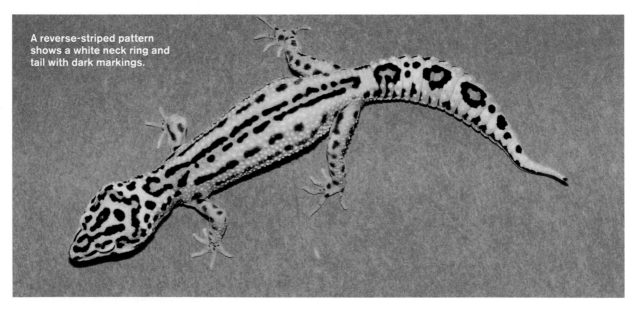

A reverse-striped pattern shows a white neck ring and tail with dark markings.

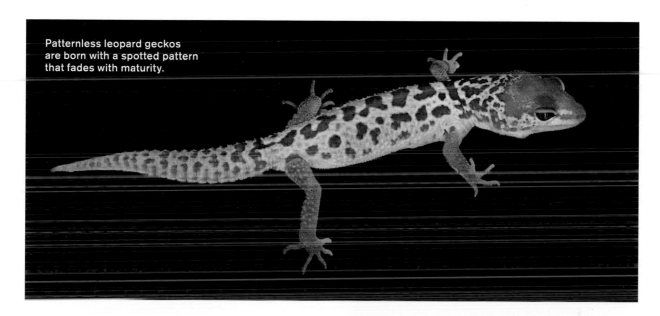

Patternless leopard geckos are born with a spotted pattern that fades with maturity.

HANDLING YOUR GECKO

Leopard geckos, even though they are among the most easily kept lizards, are not necessarily the best lizard pets to be handled and interacted with frequently. They should be thought of as display lizards that will tolerate occasional handling.

Still, leopard geckos seldom bite and, if they do, the bite is of little consequence. Also, after a little handling, leopard geckos don't scurry but instead move in a relatively slow and deliberate manner. As with all animals, the degree to which your leopard gecko interacts with you depends on the animal's genetic propensity and the amount of interaction

Did You Know?

As a general rule, closely supervise children when they are handling leopard geckos.

Did You Know?

If you are looking for a pet lizard that can tolerate longer periods of handling and more interaction, better choices are the blue-tongued skinks (*Tiliqua scincoides* and *T. gigas*) and the bearded dragon (*Pogona vitticeps*).

Notice the lack of dark markings on this adult patternless gecko.

you invest in it. If you don't spend the time getting your leopard gecko accustomed to gentle handling, it will remain skittish.

Leopard geckos that are regularly handled for short periods are usually calmer than animals that do not have such interaction. Extensive and long-term handling, however, is generally not recommended because it causes the animals stress. Hatchlings and juveniles are smaller and more nervous than adults and should not be unnecessarily handled until they become subadults of at least 5 inches long.

When picking up an adult leopard gecko, the best approach is to scoop your hand under the body

Bringing Home the Gecko

No matter where you buy your leopard gecko, be prepared to transport it home safe and sound. This is fairly easy, but if you are a first-time gecko buyer, there are a few things to remember.

The seller will put the gecko in some type of container with air holes punched in it, such as a shallow cup or a small box. If the weather is particularly cold, you can put the gecko's container inside another bag for better insulation. If the trip home is going to be a long one, consider bringing a small, insulated cooler with you to place the gecko in for the trip home. If you have someone else with you, it is a good idea to have that person warm up the car for a few minutes before taking the gecko out to it.

If it is particularly hot, run the air conditioning in the car, but don't put the gecko near the vents. Your new lizard will be fine if kept out of direct sunshine.

No matter what the weather is like, drive straight home without stopping if possible. Once home, put the gecko in its new home right away.

Leopard Geckos and Human Health

As long as you keep up with cage maintenance, a leopard gecko is a fairly clean animal. Of course, this does not mean it is totally free of germs.

Reptiles, birds, and other animals can carry salmonella. It is part of the normal bacterial flora that lives in their digestive tracts. While the chance of contracting salmonella or any other illness from a leopard gecko is remote, take sensible precautions.

Always wash your hands with soap and water after handling the gecko as well as after handling any items from its enclosure, such as the water bowl or hide box. Don't allow items from the cage to come in contact with anything—including countertops—that is used for human food preparation. If you need to use a sink or bathtub to clean the gecko's cage or accessories, clean the sink or tub with a 10 percent bleach and water solution afterward. As an extra precaution, do not let a child handle a leopard gecko unsupervised (for both the lizard's and the child's sakes).

If you follow these guidelines, you will not have to worry about any health issues resulting from keeping leopard geckos or other pet reptiles.

behind the front legs and gently close your hand. This will restrain the gecko without allowing it to bite and without causing harm—as long as you don't squeeze too tightly. Once a gecko gets used to gentle handling, it may be willing to just crawl into your palm.

You can cup a small juvenile or hatchling in your hands when you need to move it someplace, such as when cleaning the cage. An even better method is to coax it into a clean cup or other steep-sided container from which it cannot escape.

Be warned that if a leopard gecko falls from any height, it can be injured, perhaps fatally. Hold the gecko firmly and handle it only over a table or counter so if it does squirm out of your grasp and fall, the fall will be only a few inches and unlikely to cause harm.

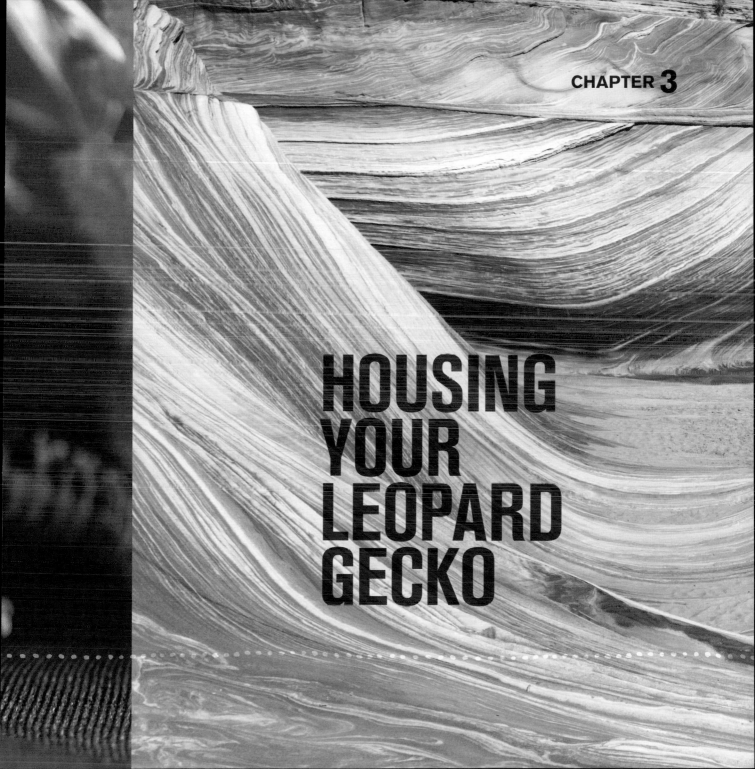

CHAPTER 3

HOUSING YOUR LEOPARD GECKO

O ne of the attributes of leopard geckos that make them good pets is their ease of care. They do quite well in simple housing but are also adaptable to more elaborate setups. As long as the pet owner meets his or her gecko's basic needs, the owner has a lot of leeway in creating the type of gecko enclosure that he or she wants.

SELECTING AN ENCLOSURE

The most commonly sold reptile enclosures in the pet trade are all-glass tanks with screen tops, but a better choice is an enclosure designed specifically for reptiles. This type of enclosure usually opens in the front with a hinged or sliding glass door. Some designs have tops that open as well, making them easily

A basic setup includes a shelter, food/water dishes, and a source of light and heat.

accessible for maintenance. They can be found in most pet stores that stock reptiles; you can also purchase them at reptile shows and online.

For display purposes, a standard 10-gallon (38-liter) aquarium or enclosure of similar size (20 x 10 inches [51 x 25 cm]) is an adequate vivarium for a single leopard gecko. A standard 20-gallon (75-liter) long aquarium or equivalent (30 x 12 inches [76 x 31 cm]) readily accommodates a pair (but never more than one male per enclosure!). Depending on space availability and the kind of design you want to incorporate into the vivarium, you may prefer a larger enclosure. A larger cage allows you more options for furnishings and live plants.

What's a Vivarium?

You are likely familiar with the word *terrarium*, meaning an enclosure for land-dwelling animals, as well as the term *aquarium*, which is an enclosure that holds water-dwelling animals. You may not be familiar with the word *vivarium*. A vivarium is an enclosure that holds an animal (or animals) in an environment that attempts to replicate their natural habitat. It includes live plants, appropriate soil, and lighting that mimics natural sunlight. Keeping herps in vivaria provides them with more opportunities to perform natural behaviors.

The senior author of this book worked to popularize vivaria within the herp-keeping community in the early 1990s. The goal was to shift the focus of hobbyists from keeping reptiles and amphibians in relatively sterile environments to keeping them in slices of the natural world. You can think of it as the philosophy of fish keeping applied to reptiles and amphibians. The emphasis is on the enclosure as a living system, as opposed to one that provides just the animal's minimum needs.

Although leopard geckos and some of the other species discussed in this book will thrive in simplistic setups, the authors encourage hobbyists to keep their pets in vivaria.

Some large-scale breeders use plastic sweater-box-type enclosures, but these don't allow for viewing. The advantage of these enclosures is that they have a low profile and fit into racks, so they allow breeders to keep more geckos in a smaller space. This type of gecko housing is unlikely to be found in a typical pet store but is available through reptile specialty retailers, at reptile expos, or through online vendors.

Although your leopard gecko is not likely to climb out of a glass enclosure without a top, a screened cover is recommended. It will allow you to safely place lights on top of the vivarium and will prevent a leopard gecko from escaping by climbing onto vivarium landscape structures, such as plants, rocks, or wood. A screen cover will also keep out the household cat or dog, prevent the escape of insect prey, and reduce the temptation for small children to handle the gecko excessively.

PLACING THE ENCLOSURE

There are not too many dos and don'ts regarding where to put your leopard gecko's home. It should be high enough off the floor to allow easy viewing but not so high as to make maintenance difficult. Standard

An albino orange leopard gecko.

fish-tank stands are often a bit too low for viewing, but they allow for easy maintenance if you have a top-opening enclosure. A wooden stand usually features a cabinet beneath the enclosure, which allows you to store equipment. With an iron stand, you can keep a smaller enclosure with more geckos or other reptiles underneath.

If you're using a piece of furniture other than a tank stand to support the enclosure, be sure it can hold the weight. This is especially important if you are using a lot of sand and rocks in your décor. It also needs to be stable and not likely to tip over. If you or someone you know is handy, building a custom stand is certainly an option.

Put the enclosure in an area of the house where people can enjoy watching the geckos. Keep in mind, though, that too much foot traffic may cause the lizards stress. Kitchens are generally not good places to keep reptiles (or other pets) because of the variations in temperature and possible fumes from ovens, cleaners, and the like.

Do not put the enclosure in a place that gets direct sunlight. A glass or acrylic enclosure will trap the heat from the sunlight like a greenhouse would, and the temperature can rise high enough to kill a leopard gecko. Similarly, try to avoid placing the cage near heating ducts and air conditioners. These devices make it difficult to keep the vivarium's temperature within the healthy range for leopard geckos.

SUBSTRATES

The substrate, sometimes called bedding, is any material that covers the floor of the enclosure. The substrate has several functions: it gives the lizard some traction so it can walk easily, it helps absorb waste until you can remove it, and it often adds to the visual appeal of the cage. Some substrates allow geckos to burrow, which is a natural behavior for them.

Leopard geckos are hardy and adaptable creatures, so a wide range of substrates will work in their housing. The choice of

Defecatorium

The next time you play a word game with your friends, surprise them with the word *defecatorium*. This is a technical term that describes regularly used defecation sites of lizards, such as leopard geckos. The plural of defecatorium is *defecatoria*. The leopard gecko is the best known of the lizards that use defecatoria and do not foul their homes. Several other eyelid geckos also use defecatoria, notably the banded geckos (genus *Coleonyx*) and the African clawed geckos (*Holodactylus africanus*).

If you choose sand as a substrate, be sure to buy a recommended brand that has little risk of impaction.

substrate is largely up to you and the type of enclosure you want to create. Factors to consider are ease of maintenance, appearance, expense, and availability. Suitable substrates include newspaper, paper towels, cage carpet, recycled paper bedding, and sand.

NEWSPAPER AND PAPER TOWELS

The first substrate choices of many breeders, particularly for baby leopard geckos, are newspaper and paper towels. These are likely the safest choices out of all the possible leopard gecko substrates. They are inexpensive, relatively sterile, and easy to monitor and replace. However, many pet owners prefer to keep their animals on a substrate that is more natural looking and pleasing to the eye.

Newspaper and paper towels need to be replaced frequently. It is likely that you will need to change the paper two to three times weekly, but it will depend on how many geckos you are housing in the cage.

Newspaper and paper towels do not allow geckos to burrow. If you opt to use one of these substrates, be sure to include numerous hiding places in the enclosure to take the place of burrows. Also be aware that feeder insects often get under the paper. Check for uneaten food beneath the paper.

CAGE CARPET

Cage carpet—also called a cage liner—is sturdy fabric, usually green or brown in color, designed for use in reptile enclosures. It works fairly well for leopard geckos and many other lizards. Cage liners are generally safe, although occasionally a little strand of the fabric unravels. This can pose a hazard by wrapping around a gecko's toe and cutting off the circulation. A keeper can prevent this by checking for loose strands whenever he or she takes the carpet out for cleaning. Simply snip off any loose threads or dispose of the whole carpet if it is too worn out.

The two drawbacks to cage carpet are the expense and the fact that they do not allow for normal burrowing behaviors. The expense of purchasing cage carpet is balanced by the fact that the carpet lasts a long time. It can be washed and reused. Have a spare on hand so that when one carpet is being washed, you can place the other in the cage. As with newspaper, feeder insects can sometimes get under the carpet. It may be difficult to find carpet that fits your cage exactly if you are not using a standard-sized aquarium or glass reptile enclosure.

Unsafe Substrates

Some substrate choices are completely unsuitable for leopard geckos. Some of these were once used as substrates but have fallen out of favor as our knowledge of proper care for these animals has grown. Others are sometimes used by keepers who have not done their research about what leopard geckos need. The following substrates have proven to be unsafe for leopard geckos:

- Alfalfa pellets
- Artificial turf/indoor-outdoor carpeting
- Calcium sand
- Corncob bedding
- Crushed walnut shells
- Gravel
- Potting soil
- Soil from outdoors
- Wood shavings

A juvenile leopard gecko.

RECYCLED PAPER BEDDING

Made from shredded, partially processed paper, recycled paper bedding is usually sold as bedding for small animals, such as rabbits and hamsters, and it works well for a variety of reptiles, too. It is usually located in the small animal section of pet-supply stores rather than in the reptile section. When using this bedding, cover the bottom of the enclosure to a depth of at least 2 inches (5 cm). It will compact over time.

The paper is soft, absorbent, long lasting, and compostable, and it allows animals to burrow into it. It can be spot cleaned because it tends to form clumps around droppings. It seems to cause little to no risk of impaction for the animals. One of the authors has used this type of substrate for more than a decade with leopard geckos, bearded dragons, and several species of snakes.

On the downside, recycled paper bedding is a bit dusty and can cause eye irritation in some reptiles (although not in leopard geckos, as far as we know). It is also one of the more expensive substrate choices. Some people find that this substrate has an unpleasant odor, and some brands of recycled paper bedding now contain baking soda as an odor-controlling agent; however, it is not known if the brands with added baking soda are safe for use with reptiles. Several of the manufacturers have not tested the product with reptiles since the addition of the baking soda, so until more research has been conducted, avoid the use of this bedding if it contains baking soda. At least one national brand was still free of baking soda as of this writing.

SAND

In the wild, leopard geckos can be found in rocky areas with clay-gravel soil covered by sand. While the first substrate choice of many breeders for leopard geckos in captivity, particularly for babies, is newspaper or paper towels because they are inexpensive, relatively sterile, and easy to monitor and replace, many pet owners prefer to keep their animals on a more natural-looking and aesthetically pleasing substrate. In these cases, the preferred choice is fine-grade sand or a mix of sand and soil. Several kinds of sand, including natural red sands, are sold in the pet trade. However, child's play sand is much cheaper and is the same sand as what is packaged for reptiles. Play sand can be found at toy, hardware, and home and garden stores.

There have been some reports of leopard geckos, mostly babies, ingesting sand and dying of sand impaction. For this reason, many breeders recommend that babies initially be kept on paper and switched

Keep your gecko's health and safety in mind when choosing a substrate for its enclosure.

over to sand later, when they have reached a length of 6 inches (a little more than 15 cm).

At the root of the impaction problem is the availability of calcium. Like many other terrestrial geckos, such as frog-eyed geckos (*Teratoscincus*) and spider geckos (*Agamura*), leopard geckos naturally ingest substrate matter as a source of calcium. Supplying calcium by coating the insects you feed your leopard gecko and offering dishes of powdered calcium supplement will usually satisfy your pet's calcium needs and prevent or reduce the ingestion of large amounts of sand.

Calcium sands are not recommended. Geckos seeking calcium will ingest this substrate, sometimes in large quantities. Although the gecko will eventually digest the calcium sand, it does so slowly. The lizard's digestion will likely not keep up with pace of ingestion. For this reason, calcium sands are more prone to causing impaction than other sands.

The grade of sand is also a significant factor in impaction; fine sands are less likely to cause impaction than coarse ones. To reduce sand ingestion when feeding, offer food insects in feeding dishes.

Place the sand in the bottom of the enclosure to a depth of about 2 to 3 inches (5 to 8 cm). Be aware that under-tank heaters may not penetrate sand well. Also, if a gecko burrows under the sand above an under-tank heater, it may become overheated. If you use sand, it is best to heat your gecko enclosure with something other than an under-tank heater.

TILES

A more recent trend in leopard gecko care is the use of ceramic, slate, and porcelain tiles as a substrate. These are safe for the gecko and conduct and retain heat exceptionally well. Unless you drop one on a hard surface and it shatters, tiles last practically forever. Another advantage of this substrate is that it will help keep a leopard gecko's nails worn down.

Choose a substrate that's easy to keep clean.

Choose tiles no thicker than about .375 inch (.95 cm); otherwise, an under-tank heater will not be able to penetrate the tile. You can purchase tiles at home and garden stores, and these stores often will cut the tiles to fit for free or a small fee. Buy extras so that you can take soiled ones out of the enclosure for cleaning and disinfecting as needed and replace them with the additional clean ones.

HEATING

Like most reptiles in captivity, leopard geckos fare best in environments that provide a heat gradient. Cold-blooded animals like leopard geckos must have warmer and cooler areas within their enclosure in order to regulate their own temperature. This is called *behavioral thermoregulation*. The availability of a heat gradient in the enclosure leads to a better growth rate and healthier geckos.

During the day, the warmest part of the enclosure should have an air temperature of 84–88°F (29–31°C). Inside the warmest shelter, 88–92°F (31–33°C) is the proper temperature. At the cool end, the temperature should be no warmer than around 75°F (24°C). At night, it's fine if the temperature drops to around 65°F (18°C), provided there is still a warmer spot in cage, such as an under-tank heater. If nighttime temperatures don't go below 75°F (24°C), you will not need to leave any heating devices turned on overnight.

THERMOMETERS

To make sure that temperatures are in the proper range, you will need thermometers. You should have one thermometer for the warm side of the cage and one for the cool side. Having additional thermometers to measure the temperature inside hide boxes, up on basking rocks, and the like is recommended.

> ### Did You Know?
> Give your gecko roughly twelve to fourteen hours of daytime temperatures each day. Setting your heating devices on timers makes this easy.

There are many types of thermometers to choose from. The most accurate are digital thermometers with external probes. These are available from electronics stores and online retailers; stores that specialize in reptiles or other exotic animals sometimes stock them as well. These digital thermometers are especially useful because they can record the highest and lowest temperatures in a twenty-four-hour period, allowing you to see the temperature extremes even if you aren't able to view the thermometer at those times.

The thin plastic strips that stick on the side of the glass are not accurate, so don't choose this type of thermometer for your gecko's enclosure. The dial type of thermometer is better than the strips but less accurate than a digital thermometer.

Another option is an infrared temperature gun. This is not a thermometer; rather, this device records the temperature of a place or object at which you point it, such as a basking rock, a hide box, or the lizard itself. Infrared temperature guns are highly accurate and take only a second or two to produce a reading. This is an especially useful device for monitoring temperatures if you have a number of reptile enclosures. Look for them online or at reptile shows.

REPTILE HEATING PADS AND HEAT TAPE

The most common types of heating pads are under-tank heating pads, which, as the name suggests, are placed under reptile enclosures. If used properly, these are effective heating systems for leopard gecko enclosures lined with paper or with thin (1 inch [2.5 cm] or less) layers of substrate. If the substrate is several inches thick, it will act as insulation, preventing the heat from rising and causing it to build up to high levels at the bottom of the tank.

Select a heating unit that covers 25 to 35 percent of the enclosure's floor area. It is critical that most of the floor area be unheated to allow the animals to thermoregulate. To prevent mishaps, such as electrocution or overheating, follow manufacturer instructions carefully.

Did You Know?

Modern reptile under-tank heating pads do not get hot enough to burn leopard geckos unless malfunctioning. Use of a thermostat for these devices is not necessary but is wise.

When using an under-tank heater, raise the bottom of the enclosure slightly to allow for airflow between the tank and the heater. If enclosures with recessed glass bottoms (most glass enclosures have recessed bottoms) do not have sufficient airflow, heat can build up within the air space and cause the bottom of the tank to crack.

Another option is heat tape. You must connect heat tape to a thermostat to ensure it does not produce too much heat.

INCANDESCENT BULBS

Some leopard gecko specialists choose to heat enclosures with incandescent bulbs in reflector-type fixtures placed on top of screen covers or anchored above open-top enclosures. For most enclosures, a 40- or 60-watt bulb provides the desired heat range for leopard geckos. To ensure the correct temperature, use a

thermometer to measure the temperature of the heated ground area closest to the bulb. The thermometer should read 84–88°F (29–31°C).

Incandescent fixtures are best used on vivaria that are at least 24 inches (61 cm) long with fully ventilated tops. With smaller enclosures, there may not be enough surface area to create a temperature gradient that includes a cool area, causing an increased risk of overheating. Remember, the purpose of providing heat is to allow a lizard to thermoregulate by moving between a heat source and a cooler, unheated area.

HOT ROCKS

Although pet stores often recommend hot-rock heating systems, these types of heaters are not appropriate for vivaria. The primary problem is with the surface temperature of hot rocks because some simply get too hot (up to 105°F [41°C]), and others have hot spots. All hot rocks can cause an unnatural temperature gradient, creating a small, hot surface with the rest of the vivarium remaining too cool. This can burn a leopard gecko and cause skin damage on the belly area because the gecko must lie on a hot surface for extended periods of time to keep warm. Many reptiles have died because of hot rocks, so their use is not recommended.

A Good Hot Rock

Hot rocks manufactured for use with reptiles are not recommended for your leopard gecko's enclosure, but you can make your own hot rock to serve as a natural warm spot for your lizard. In nature, geckos and other reptiles will lie on rocks that are warmed by the hot rays of the sun during the day and that stay warm for several hours into the night. It's easy to set up a similar situation in your gecko's enclosure.

You will need a basking light and a flat, preferably dark-colored, rock. Dark-colored rocks will absorb heat better than light-colored ones. Different types of rock absorb heat better than others, so you may want to experiment with various rocks.

Place the rock on the substrate directly under the basking lamp. It will sit there all day, absorbing heat from the basking bulb. When the lights are turned off, the rock will radiate warmth, and your gecko can use it to warm up at night. This is not a substitute for maintaining proper cage temperatures, but it provides some supplemental heat in a form that the gecko would encounter in nature.

HEATING SAFETY

Every year, herpetoculture products, including spotlights in reflector-type fixtures or heating units, cause fires. The fires are caused by pets toppling lights, lights being placed too close to flammable materials, or heating units malfunctioning. Space heaters can wipe out an entire collection of reptiles if the thermostat fails or is poorly adjusted.

Think safety when keeping reptiles. Consider every possible scenario and make necessary adjustments. Here are some important guidelines to remember.

- Do not allow any pets to wander free in a room with incandescent heat bulbs or space heaters; cats are especially prone to knocking over heat lamps.
- Closely monitor children around enclosures.
- Install a smoke detector in any room with heating and lighting products.
- Connect space heaters with backup thermostats.
- Consider a digital thermometer or thermostat system with an alarm that will warn you if a temperature exceeds a particular setting. Such a system can be expensive, but it could prove a lifesaver for large-scale reptile operations.

RELATIVE AIR HUMIDITY

Herpetoculturists specializing in geckos have confirmed the benefits of increasing air humidity within the shelters of ground-dwelling geckos, with the primary goals being to reduce the rate of dehydration and to facilitate shedding, which contributes to the animals' overall health. Leopard geckos fare best when provided with at least one humidified shelter. This is especially true if you live in a dry area or have central air conditioning in your home, which tends to keep relative humidity low.

If you are using sand or recycled paper bedding as a ground medium, simply wet the medium beneath the shelter(s) once or twice a week to provide enough relative humidity for the well-being of your geckos. Another practice is to use an oversized shelter with a small container holding a mixture of moistened sand and vermiculite (a common potting mix) placed in the center. Regularly monitor and water the container to maintain its moisture level. These procedures are particularly beneficial for hatchlings and juveniles.

If you live in a dry region, try using a small plastic food-storage container with a hole cut out of the side as a humidified shelter. Line the bottom of the shelter with a substrate of slightly moist foam sponge. When using this kind of humidified shelter, always include an additional dry shelter in your setup.

SHELTERS

Leopard geckos are nocturnal animals that usually avoid bright light and try to remain concealed from potential predators. In the wild, they spend a great deal of their time out of sight and inside various forms of shelter, such as burrows or rock crevices. For this reason, it is essential to provide your pet leopard gecko with some form of shelter, often called *hide boxes* and *hides* by hobbyists.

Commercially made reptile shelters range from basic plastic boxes to molded concrete or plastic structures that resemble rock or bark and work well with leopard geckos. Many other landscape products

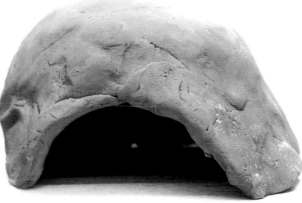

currently sold in the trade, such as cork bark, dried woods, and rock, are ideal for creating natural-looking shelters.

Be extremely careful when using heavy materials, such as rock or wood, in creating shelters as well as when lifting or removing them. Position them securely, with no risk of toppling, which could crush or injure a gecko. Use silicone glue to help anchor pieces together.

MAINTENANCE

Leopard gecko enclosures are easy to maintain because leopard geckos are essentially clean animals that will defecate in a specific location of the vivarium. In addition, their stools are relatively dry and easy to scoop out. Scoop feces every week and replace the substrate as needed.

Don't allow the enclosure to get wet and be sure to provide adequate ventilation. Ammonia is produced when water combines with the uric acid of the feces. If you do not remove the feces, the ammonia can have harmful effects on the lizard's eyes, skin, and respiratory system, particularly in an unventilated plastic sweater-box type of container. Excess moisture in unventilated enclosures can also lead to infections of the skin and digits. If you keep leopard geckos in such enclosures in large numbers (which is unlikely for the typical pet owner), you must soak all containers in a bleach solution at least twice a year.

Sometimes, the food bowl becomes a place to relax.

Inspect your gecko's enclosure every day. Check that the temperatures are correct and that the humidified hide boxes are still moist. If you are using newspaper or paper towels as your substrate, check to see if it needs to be replaced. Dump the water bowl and give your gecko fresh water two to three times per week—or more often if you find any substrate, fecal matter, drowned feeder insects, or other foreign matter in the water. Clean out the food bowl as needed.

Disinfecting for Gecko Keepers

Many keepers like to bring interesting rocks and pieces of wood in from the outdoors for use in their reptile enclosures. There is nothing wrong with this practice, but keepers must clean and disinfect these items before placing them in their animals' enclosures. Any parasites or pathogens living on these items must be eliminated as thoroughly as possible. Some experts even recommend disinfecting store-bought items or any used items you purchase.

Before you can disinfect an item, it has to be clean. Disinfection is less effective if there is dirt, fungi, and other material stuck to the item. Wash the item in hot water, cleaning out all nooks and crannies. You may want to use a toothbrush, pipe cleaners, or toothpicks to get into all of the small places. Rinse the item thoroughly and allow it to air dry.

After the item dries, you can disinfect it. The most common way to disinfect items used in reptile enclosures is with bleach; it is readily available, inexpensive, and—when used properly—relatively safe. It kills a wide range of pathogens. Use plain, ordinary bleach without any scents, detergents, or other chemicals.

Wear gloves when working with bleach to avoid skin irritation; goggles are also recommended. Work with bleach only in a well-ventilated area or outdoors.

To disinfect, make a solution of 10 percent bleach: use 9 parts water to 1 part bleach. Make enough to immerse the item or items you are disinfecting. If you are disinfecting an enclosure or particularly large items, you can put the solution in a spray bottle and spray it on the items to be disinfected. Be sure to label the bottle as containing bleach and use the bottle only for the purpose of disinfecting.

Completely immerse the item in the bleach solution. If using the spray bottle, mist the item or enclosure thoroughly with the solution so that it is soaked. After fifteen minutes or longer, rinse the item thoroughly several times with fresh water until there is no bleach smell left on the item. Let it air dry, preferably in direct sunlight. Once dry, it's ready to use.

At least once a week, wipe down the walls of the enclosure with a damp rag or paper towels to remove any dirt or smudges. If there is something stuck on the glass, use white vinegar for safe and effective cleaning.

Two or three times a year, clean and disinfect all items in your gecko's enclosure. You can clean and disinfect your gecko's gear in a bathtub or outdoors, depending on your preference. If using your bathtub, be sure to clean and disinfect the tub afterward to prevent the unlikely occurrence of passing salmonella to other members of the household.

Scrub each item thoroughly, removing any fecal matter, dirt, or grime. You can use any mild, unscented soap. Thoroughly rinse the items and then disinfect them with a 10 percent bleach solution. Allow the items to soak in a bucket or tub of the bleach solution for fifteen to thirty minutes. Afterward, rinse them until no bleach smell remains and then allow them to air dry. You can put some items, such as the food and water bowls, in the dishwasher rather than soaking them in bleach.

While you are cleaning and disinfecting your leopard gecko's accessories, clean and disinfect the cage as well. Start by putting your leopard gecko in a safe location, such as a small aquarium set aside for this purpose. Next, remove the substrate. If you use sand or recycled paper bedding, scoop it all out and then use a vacuum cleaner to suck up the remaining dust.

Wash the enclosure with hot water to remove all waste material and then wipe it down or spray it with a bleach solution. Let the bleach sit on the cage for fifteen to thirty minutes and then rinse the enclosure with plain water until no bleach smell remains. Dry it off with paper towels or allow it to air dry. Once the enclosure is dry, add clean substrate and replace the disinfected furnishings. Once everything is back in its place, you can return your leopard gecko to its home.

When doing this major cleaning and disinfecting, it's a good time to also dust the light fixtures and power strips, clean under and around the cage, clean the tank stand, and so forth. Check your power cords, light fixtures, cage furnishings, and all other items for any signs of wear or damage. Replace anything that isn't in excellent condition.

NATURALISTIC VIVARIUM DESIGN

The first time that the senior author ever saw a leopard gecko was in Paris, France, in 1962. It lived in an 80-gallon (303-liter) planted community vivarium with African flat lizards (*Platysaurus* sp.), a giant day gecko (*Phelsuma* sp.), and a Brazilian monkey frog (*Phyllomedusa rohdei*). The leopard gecko lived in the dry half of the enclosure. The author had the opportunity to observe the vivarium and the behaviors of the various lizards for several hours at a time, and this experience planted the seed for his interest in naturalistic vivarium design.

A leopard gecko can fare well in an enclosure with a simple substrate, a shelter, and a shallow water container, but if you want to observe a wider range of gecko behaviors, purchase a larger enclosure and design a naturalistic vivarium. Given the opportunity, leopard geckos will display a greater range of activities in a more three-dimensional environment.

Leopard geckos thrive in environments that mimic their natural habitats.

The following information is designed to introduce readers to this alternative method of keeping reptiles, which the authors believe is much more rewarding, interesting, and aesthetically pleasing than the utilitarian approach taken by most breeders. However, if naturalistic vivaria are not carefully planned and designed, they can offer a higher probability of risks that can lead to accidental injury or death than simple laboratory-type setups. For this reason, they are not recommended for housing valuable breeder animals. However, careful attention to design can significantly reduce any risks.

ENCLOSURES

The minimum size for a naturalistic vivarium for leopard geckos is 36 inches (91 cm) long with a screen top. Larger enclosures allow for even more interesting designs; the senior author prefers 48-inch-long (122-cm-long) vivaria. A front-opening enclosure is best because it allows you easy access to the interior.

Avoid using a thin glass enclosure because the bottom may fall out after you introduce landscape structures. A plastic-sided enclosure with a screen top can work well.

SUBSTRATE

Cover the bottom of the enclosure with a drainage layer to a depth of about 2 inches. While gravel was formerly the drainage layer of choice, it makes the vivarium very heavy and has fallen out of favor as better materials have come along. The most commonly used drainage layer is expanded clay aggregate, which is lightweight and safe to use. Put a fine mesh screen on top of the drainage layer to prevent the substrate from sinking down into the drainage layer.

On top of the mesh screen, add a sand and soil blend consisting of two parts sand and one part soil to a depth of about 3 inches. Use an organic soil that does not contain added fertilizers or perlite. You can also buy soil designed for use in reptile vivaria from reptile-supply and vivarium-supply companies.

You can use natural wood in vivarium landscaping.

LANDSCAPING

Rocks will create natural-looking shelters and climbing areas. A word of warning about rocks, though: a good-looking setup requires a lot of them. The senior author once had a beautiful 80-gallon (303-liter) leopard gecko vivarium that fell apart when 230 pounds (104 kg) of rock and 120 pounds (54.5 kg) of substrate fell through the bottom. Fortunately, no animals were hurt, but it did teach the author a lesson about landscaping desert vivaria.

There are alternatives to using heavy rocks or thick layers of substrate, such as using broad sections of wood, which are much lighter than granite or limestone. He recommends cork bark slabs and sculptured, sandblasted fig wood or grape wood, which are available in many reptile specialty stores. Combining wood with sections of cork bark gives a nice effect and makes it easy to create shelves and shelters.

If using rock is important to you, you can make artificial rock landscaping by using polystyrene foam plastic as a core and then surrounding it with concrete. For more natural colors, add concrete dyes to the mix. Another alternative is to mix concrete with soil or peat moss and hand-form light, rocklike structures.

Combine a few rocks with select pieces of wood, limiting the weight of the rock and wood to no more than the size of the vivarium (for example, 80 pounds [36 kg] for an 80-gallon [303-liter] vivarium). Because 1.5 to 2 pounds per gallon (.68 to .91 kg) of substrate is required for a decent layer, the total weight of

A coconut shell provides a visually interesting hiding spot for your gecko.

landscape structures for an 80-gallon (303-liter) tank can exceed 200 pounds (91 kg). Distribute the landscaping over a wide area so that the weight is not concentrated in the center.

Form ground-level shelters and basking sites by overlapping flattened rocks or safer cork bark sections. You can make ramps that allow a gecko to climb from ground level to elevated sites with sections of bark or thick wood. With overhanging shelters, you can observe your gecko(s) sleeping during the day. A broad overhang provides enough shade from overhead lights that a leopard gecko will not mind resting under the overhang during the day.

PLANTS

A major reason to create a vivarium is to house leopard geckos and live plants together. Many gecko keepers enjoy creating small slices of nature in the comfort of their own living rooms. Plants are important parts of their vivaria.

Plants for a leopard gecko enclosure must be tolerant of desertlike conditions. They must also stand up to being climbed on by the geckos.

Snake plants (*Sansevieria* sp.) come in a variety of shapes and sizes and can be introduced in broad, shallow pots buried in the substrate or planted directly in a sand-and-soil substrate mix behind landscape structures. Small ponytailed palms (*Beaucarnea recurvata*) with grasslike leaves also thrive in this kind of vivarium. Other choices include the succulent philodendron (*Zamiaculcas zamiifolia*, which fares well in bright shade), haworthia (*Hathworthia*), climbing aloe (*Aloe ciliaris*), and caudexed fig (*Ficus petiolaris*).

One of the few cacti to work consistently well in vivaria is the padded and nearly spineless tree opuntia (*Consolea falcate*). Good levels of daytime lighting (two to four fluorescent bulbs) are a must to keep them thriving. These plants can be ordered from cactus and succulent nurseries. There are also companies that provide plants specifically for use in reptile and amphibian enclosures, but most of these cater to dart-frog keepers so may not have a great selection of desert plants.

When including the plants, consider how plants occur in nature. Look at pictures of deserts online to see how and where the plants grow in relation to rocks and each other. For example, plants of the same type are often found in little clumps. Most vivarium keepers strive to create natural-looking settings, but you can do as you like as long as your choices are safe for the animals.

A collared lizard.

OTHER ANIMALS

In large vivaria, it is possible to keep other lizards with adult leopard geckos. The senior author has successfully maintained pairs of collared lizards (*Crotaphytus* sp.) with these geckos. South African flat lizards (*Platysaurus* sp.) and small girdle-tailed lizards (*Cordylus* sp.) can also be kept successfully with leopard geckos.

The lizards in a combined vivarium should be approximately the same size and have different niche requirements (e.g., collared lizards are active during the day and leopard geckos are active at night). They should, however, come from habitats with similar climatic and geographic/topographic characteristics (e.g., desert/moderate relative humidity with daytime highs in the high 80s to low 90s Fahrenheit [low 30s Celsius] and nighttime temperatures in the 70s [low to mid-20s Celsius], with a combination of rock and sandy soil substrate).

All individuals should be quarantined and evaluated for disease prior to their introduction into a community vivarium. Remember to keep a close eye on mixed vivaria. While some species will fare well together, others have to be removed when a problem is detected.

LIGHTS AND HEATING

Use two full-spectrum fluorescent bulbs running the length of the enclosure for growing plants and general light quality. If diurnal basking lizards, such as collared lizards and armadillo lizards, are kept in the same vivarium as leopard geckos, they will require a light that produces ultraviolet B (UVB) waves. In this case, substitute a UVB bulb for one of the full-spectrum bulbs. To make sure you are lighting these other species correctly, consult an authoritative source on their care.

In 48-inch-long (122-cm-long) and larger enclosures, place one or two spotlights over an area of stacked rock or wood to provide a basking area. If leopard geckos are kept alone, the basking area should be

Quarantine

No matter how careful you are when selecting a new leopard gecko, there is always a chance that your new lizard is sick. Reptiles are masters at hiding illnesses until they are practically at death's door.

To prevent your new lizard from infecting your other reptiles with a disease, you should place it in quarantine. Even if you don't have other reptiles, quarantining a new gecko is smart because it allows you to observe the lizard closely and helps prevent a sick animal from introducing illness to the main enclosure. You should quarantine any lizard that is new to you, regardless of where you obtained it. Quarantine is especially critical if the new lizard is wild-caught, as will likely be the case if you eventually decide to keep some of the rarer eyelid geckos.

A quarantine setup is a separate enclosure used to house a gecko for several weeks when it is first obtained. Ideally, you should keep the quarantine enclosure in a room that has no other reptiles in it. If that is not possible, station it as far as possible from other reptile enclosures.

Keep the quarantine cage simple so that it is easy for you to see the gecko and maintain the enclosure. However, the setup needs to provide the proper environment for the gecko. Set up the heating as you would normally. Use paper towels as the substrate because they are easy to clean up and they show feces well, so you can spot any digestive problems your gecko may have. Mites also show up well on paper towels. For shelters, you can use plastic food storage containers, plastic reptile hide boxes, or other items that are easy to clean or that can be discarded after use.

Care for a gecko in quarantine as you normally would. Observe the animal closely. Look for any signs of health problems. If you notice that something is wrong, act quickly to remedy the problem, seeking veterinary care if needed.

An effective quarantine period lasts eight to twelve weeks. After this period, if all is well, you can move the new gecko to its permanent home. Clean and disinfect the quarantine enclosure so it's ready when you need it again.

maintained at 85–90°F (29–32°C); if kept with diurnal friends, the basking area should be 90–95°F (32–35°C) when measured at the area closest to the light. Keep the lights on for fourteen hours a day, except during two to three winter months, when you should reduce daylight hours to ten hours a day to simulate winter. At night, use one or two 25-watt red bulbs to provide mild heat and to allow observation of the lizards' nocturnal activity. Place the lights on timers to keep the photoperiod stable. Regularly check the vivarium's thermometers for correct temperatures.

Do Leopard Geckos Need UVB?

It has been assumed for quite a long time that nocturnal reptiles and amphibians—unlike their diurnal cousins—do not need exposure to UVB waves of light for optimal health. More recent observations of both wild and captive herps have cast doubt on that assumption.

Herpetologists studying nocturnal geckos in nature have observed that as the sun is rising and setting, some species of gecko will emerge and sit for a short time in the sun. Some will remain mostly hidden but allow their tails or legs to protrude into sunlight. It is believed that they do this to absorb the ultraviolet light of the sun.

Many keepers of pet nocturnal herps now include UVB-generating lighting in their enclosures. The enclosures still provide normal photoperiods, but the geckos have access to UVB if they choose. Anecdotally, keepers who provide UVB lighting claim that their animals are healthier overall, have less incidence of metabolic bone disease, and experience more breeding success.

There is not yet enough evidence to say whether geckos and other nocturnal herps benefit from UVB and how great the benefits, if any, are. If you choose to include UVB lighting, make sure your leopard gecko has a few shelters in its vivarium that allow it to get completely out of the light. Also, it is probably a good idea to use supplements that do not contain vitamin D. UVB causes animals to manufacture their own vitamin D, so there is a risk of toxicity if they are also getting vitamin D in their diets.

If you include UVB lighting in your gecko's enclosure, share what you observe with the herp-keeping community. This is an area of leopard gecko keeping in which there is still something to learn, and everyday keepers can contribute to the body of knowledge.

MAINTENANCE

The plants should be watered once or twice a week as needed. To keep the vivarium attractive, wipe the glass sides clean once a week, using white vinegar on a paper towel, followed by a rinse with distilled or purified water. Wipe the sides dry to avoid elevating the humidity in the vivarium too much. Check the lights, timers, and thermometers regularly to ensure proper working order.

Leopard Gecko Supply Checklist

- Properly sized enclosure
- Materials for drainage layer and substrate
- Heating device (under-tank heater and/or basking light)
- Hide boxes (two minimum)
- Thermometers (two recommended)
- Water bowl
- Food bowl
- Vitamin/mineral supplement (see Chapter 4)
- Live feeder insects (see Chapter 4)

FEEDING AND NUTRITION

Leopard geckos are primarily insectivorous, meaning that they typically feed on live, moving insect prey. This means that a gecko keeper will need to supply his or her animals with live insects on a regular basis. Most leopard geckos will not be interested in food that does not move. The movement of the insect attracts the gecko's attention and stimulates the gecko to hunt its prey. While there are some options for nonliving food, not all leopard geckos will accept them, and such food is not a natural diet for a leopard gecko. New gecko owners should plan on providing a live-insect diet.

The insect that gecko keepers most commonly feed their pets is the cricket. Crickets are raised in vast numbers to supply the pet trade. They are cheaply and readily available at most pet stores. Other options for live prey include mealworms, roaches, silkworms, and newborn (pinky) mice. Although it is not strictly necessary, it is a good practice to occasionally offer pet leopard geckos prey other than crickets.

As a general rule, any food items, including crickets, other insects, and pinky mice, should be no longer than the length of the lizard's head and less than half of its width. If the food is much smaller than that,

it may not attract the gecko's interest and, even if it does, it won't provide much of a meal. If the prey is larger, it may frighten the gecko or possibly injure the lizard if it does decide to eat it. Most prey items are available in a range of sizes, so it is usually not difficult to find the right size prey for any age or size of leopard gecko.

Before the consistent availability of commercially raised crickets, many herpetoculturists successfully maintained their lizards on diets consisting primarily of mealworms. However, it was difficult to achieve consistent breeding results and raise hatchlings until herpetoculturists started feeding insects that had been gut-loaded (fed a nutritional meal prior to offering—more on this practice later in the chapter) and dusted with a powdered vitamin/mineral mix.

DIET SELECTION

The best diet for leopard geckos consists of appropriately sized, commercially raised crickets, roaches, and/or mealworms. To vary the adult diet, occasionally include pinky mice, wax worms, king mealworms, and other prey in small amounts.

CRICKETS

Crickets are the most common staple food for leopard geckos—and most other insect-eating pets—and for good reason. They have proven over the decades to be easy to raise commercially, nutritious when properly cared for, accepted as prey by a wide range of insectivorous pets, and not too disagreeable to humans.

Pet stores often stock crickets in several sizes. The smallest size available is called a *pinhead* for obvious reasons. These are too small for even hatchling leopard geckos. Two-week-old crickets—often called *fly-sized*—should be the right size for hatchlings. Adult leopard geckos can take full-grown crickets. When in doubt, stick to the previously mentioned rule of thumb about the size of the prey compared to the size of the gecko's head. Do not be shy about asking to see the size of crickets or other prey available at your pet-supply store when you are deciding which size to buy.

Because you will need to feed the crickets prior to feeding them to your leopard gecko, you will

Live insects are the best prey choices for leopard geckos.

Full-sized crickets are suitable only for adult leopard geckos.

need some kind of container to keep them in for a day or two. A 2.5-gallon (9.5-liter) tank works very well for this, as do the plastic "critter keepers" and small containers designed specifically for keeping crickets that most pet stores sell. The cricket containers come with feeding tubes to make transferring the crickets from their enclosure to the leopard gecko's easier.

You may wish to keep a large number of crickets on hand to avoid having to run to the pet store frequently; this is helpful, especially if you are keeping multiple leopard geckos and plan to breed them. In this case, you will need a larger container. Plastic storage tubs and plastic garbage cans can be modified to make good cricket containers.

Whatever enclosure you choose for housing your crickets, it needs to be well ventilated and escape-proof. A screen top is usually sufficient, as are the lids that already come with the critter keepers. If you are making your own container from a storage tub or garbage can, you will need fine screening to keep the crickets inside while providing sufficient airflow.

Crickets will survive at warmer room temperatures, but they do best and grow fastest at about 80°F (27°C). They require some hiding areas in their enclosure; paper-towel and toilet-paper rolls work well for this. If you order your crickets in bulk, they will normally come with a cardboard egg crate, which can also provide hiding places. Crumpled newspaper is an option, but it can be difficult to extract the crickets from it without some escaping.

For information on feeding crickets, see the section on gut-loading later in this chapter. The best way to provide water is to give the crickets a few slices of orange, sweet potato, carrot, or apple; pieces of diced leafy greens or broccoli stems; or similar items. Put the fruits and vegetables on a piece of cardboard or in a shallow receptacle, such as a jar lid. Another option is to blend a few different fruits and vegetables into a smoothie and give it to the crickets in a jar lid or very shallow bowl. Add more fruits and vegetables as needed and remove any dried-out pieces so that the crickets always have water available.

Another option is to offer water in gelatin form, which is commercially available for crickets and other feeder insects. Water bowls are not a good idea because the crickets will crawl into the water bowls and drown.

Keep the bottom of the crickets' enclosure bare for easy cleaning. To clean the enclosure between batches of crickets, start by dumping out the cricket droppings and old food. If the bottom has any caked on dirt, wash it out with hot water. Once every couple of months, use a 10 percent bleach solution to disinfect the cricket cage as described in Chapter 3.

Feed crickets to your leopard geckos by putting a few in the geckos' enclosure. Putting them in a shallow bowl will give the geckos slightly more time to find them. The geckos will quickly see them and stalk them. Crickets have been known to bite leopard geckos and other lizards if left in the vivarium too long. To prevent this, remove any uneaten crickets from the cage after twenty-four hours.

MEALWORMS AND KING MEALWORMS

Mealworms are another readily available feeder insect for leopard geckos, and two kinds are usually available: the larval forms of two different species of darkling beetle. There is the regular mealworm, *Tenebrio molitor*, which is the smaller and more common of the two. The other is the king mealworm, *Zophobas morio*. Regular mealworms are very easy to keep and even culture, but culturing the king mealworm is more labor intensive and not worth the effort for the average gecko keeper.

Mealworms

Mealworms are small prey, typically reaching up to an inch (2.5 cm) long before going through pupation and becoming adult beetles. They are granary pests found in a variety of grains. While they are sometimes used as the staple diet for leopard geckos, they seem to be more difficult to digest than other options and may not provide lizards with a balanced diet on their own. However, they do make excellent additions to a leopard gecko's diet. They are so easy

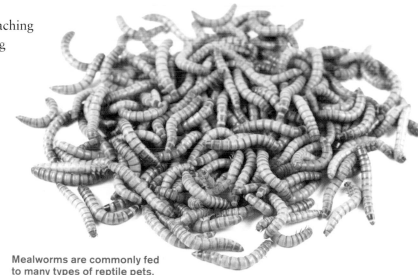

Mealworms are commonly fed to many types of reptile pets.

to maintain that it is a good idea to keep a small colony on hand for times when the local pet store is out of crickets or you are unable to get the pet store.

To set up a small culture of mealworms, you will need a container, a deep layer of mealworm food (grains), and either some damp paper towels or some pieces of moist vegetables and fruits. The container does not need a lid because both the larvae and the adults will stay in the food. Mealworms will thrive in grains. A mix of oatmeal and wheat bran works well, but almost any grain or flour will do. Place the fruit and vegetable pieces (e.g., carrots, sweet potatoes, oranges) or the damp paper towels on top for moisture. You will need to change them daily to prevent mold. Mealworms will also be fine for several days without any moisture. They really are extremely easy to keep.

Mealworms are generally sold in cups of bran in small quantities. When you bring them home, you can dump them right into the container you've set up. You can remove any dead mealworms, but you don't have to; it doesn't seem to make a difference in starting the colony. Given enough time, the mealworms will grow into adults and reproduce. If you are using them only as occasional feeders, you will build up a sustainable colony fairly quickly.

Feed mealworms to your gecko in a shallow bowl. If you just dump them into the cage, the mealworms will rapidly burrow under the substrate, and the gecko may not find them.

King Mealworms

King mealworms, also known as superworms, make a hearty meal for adult leopard geckos. They can grow to be about 2.25 inches (almost 6 cm) long before transforming into adult beetles. Young king mealworms will thrive when kept in the same type of setup as the common mealworm, but they do not readily turn into adults under the same conditions. To become adults, they need to be housed individually, which takes up too much space and time for most reptile keepers. It is far easier to buy a bunch, keep them in a container of food, and feed them to the geckos as needed.

King mealworms are best fed individually to a gecko using forceps. You can put them in a shallow bowl like you would with regular mealworms, but king mealworms are typically better able to climb out. Like mealworms, they will burrow into the substrate.

Sometimes, a king mealworm lost in the substrate will go through pupation and emerge as a large adult beetle. The beetles are not harmful, but because of their strong chemical scent, most leopard geckos will

Giant Mealworms

A feeder insect called the giant mealworm is occasionally available. It is not to be confused with the king mealworm. Giant mealworms are common mealworms treated with hormones that cause them to continue to grow without turning into adults. They are larger than untreated mealworms but not as large as king mealworms.

not eat them. Most other reptiles, as well as amphibians and fish, will also not eat them, so it's best to just dispose of them quickly.

COCKROACHES

Many keepers are disgusted by the idea of using cockroaches as feeders, and this is a shame. Domestically cultured cockroaches are clean, highly nutritious, and eagerly accepted by leopard geckos and many other herps. The species being cultured as feeder insects are all tropical, so the risk of them infesting the home is almost nonexistent (unless you live in Florida or another semitropical locale).

You can keep roaches much like you would crickets. One difference is that roaches do best at warmer temperatures. If you want to maintain a roach colony, use a small under-tank heating pad to keep your roach enclosure at around 85°F (29°C). If you are keeping the roaches for just a day or two to gut-load them before feeding them to your gecko, you don't need to heat the enclosure. Because roaches are larger than crickets, you will need a 10-gallon (38-liter) aquarium or something of similar size if you want to set up a colony of them.

Some cockroach species can climb glass. To prevent escapes, avoid those species. Luckily, two common feeder species are unable to climb glass or smooth plastic surfaces: the orange-spotted roach, *Blaptica dubia*, and the orange-headed roach, *Eublaberus prosticus*. The

Cockroaches and dubia roaches (shown) are easy to keep and gut-load.

orange-spotted can reach a length of nearly 2 inches (5 cm), while the orange-headed can grow to slightly more than 2 inches (5 cm) long. Adults may be too big for leopard geckos, but juvenile roaches make great prey.

Orange-spotted roaches—often called *dubia roaches* or *dubias*—have become widely available in the past few years and are now even available at the large chain pet stores. Orange-headed roaches and other species may be ordered online or found at reptile shows. These two species are larger than crickets and provide more nutrients per insect. If you are feeding roaches heavily, provide fewer individual insects per feeding.

The roaches available as feeders eat almost anything (which is probably not surprising), so they are easy to keep and gut-load (see section on gut-loading that follows). As with crickets, it is best to provide moisture to roaches in the form of juicy fruits and vegetables, such as sweet potatoes, apples, diced leafy greens, oranges, beets, and others. Orange-headed roaches need more protein in their diet than dubias do, so add some dry dog or cat kibble or commercially available roach food to their diet to supply the needed protein.

A few other roach species are available through pet stores and reptile suppliers. As long as they are of the appropriate size, they are fine to feed to leopard geckos.

You can feed roaches to your geckos by either letting a few loose in the cage or offering them individually with forceps, which will prevent any escapes.

OTHER OPTIONS

Numerous other prey species are available in the herp hobby. They are mostly suitable as occasional treats rather than as staple diets. None of the following are easy for the average hobbyist to cultivate, so you should buy them in small quantities as needed. Unless otherwise noted, the best method for feeding these insects to leopard geckos is in a shallow bowl.

Black Soldier Fly Larvae

Black soldier fly larvae (BSFL), *Hermetia illucens*, are one of the more exciting feeder insects to come on the herp scene. The most common and well-known brand of BSFL is sold under the name Phoenix Worms. Other brands vary in quality. BSFL are white grubs that wiggle a lot but cannot climb up the sides of most surfaces. Their wiggling incites an enthusiastic feeding response in leopard geckos and most other lizards.

A leopard gecko eats a mealworm.

The reason BSFL are exciting feeders is because of their high nutrient content and ideal ratio of calcium to phosphorus. You do not have to add any supplements when feeding BSFL. BSFL can be used as a staple diet, although due to their small size, it takes quite a few to make a full meal for an adult leopard gecko.

Keep these feeders in the cups they come in. BSFL do not need to be fed, but they do need to be kept cool. Ideally, they should be kept at around 60°F (16°C). You can keep them in a basement or in a cooler with a small ice pack to maintain them at the proper temperature. The grubs will pupate into adult flies if kept at warmer temperatures. Leopard geckos are not very good at catching flies, but the adults can be used as food for other animals that are able to catch them, such as anoles, tree frogs, and chameleons; many freshwater fish will also eat them.

Butterworms

Like mealworms—and all of the other worms discussed in this chapter—butterworms are not actually worms. They are the larvae of another insect. Specifically, butterworms are the caterpillars of the Chilean moth, *Chilecomadia moorei*. They are sometimes sold under the names *trevo worm* or *tebo worm*.

Butterworms are usually between 1.25 and 1.5 inches (3.18–3.81 cm) long. They are bright yellow in appearance, and most lizards find the color, scent, and/or movement of butterworms very enticing. Lizards that are reluctant to eat will often eagerly consume them. They are high in fat and calcium, making them a great food for underweight geckos and breeding females.

These insects come packed in containers with wheat bran. You can leave them in the containers and refrigerate them. They will last up to a month in these conditions. If you are going to feed them to your leopard gecko faster than that, you can keep them in a small container with wheat bran and thick slices of sweet potatoes. The worms will burrow into the sweet potatoes, although it is unclear if they actually eat it.

Feed your leopard geckos the butterworms in a shallow dish or individually by forceps. If placed in the gecko's enclosure, the butterworms will burrow under the substrate.

Tomato Hornworms

These caterpillars are the bright green larvae of the five-spotted hawkmoth, *Manduca quinquemaculata*. In the garden, they are pests on tomatoes and related plants. Because they eat plants with noxious or toxic foliage, only feed commercially cultured hornworms to your geckos.

Hornworms start small and grow to more than 3 inches (around 7.5 cm) long before spinning cocoons and turning into adult moths. The younger and smaller hornworms are appropriately sized for leopard geckos, and they are meaty, nutritious feeders. You do not have to feed many to make a good meal for a leopard gecko.

Hornworms come in containers with their food. Keep them in these containers at room temperature until you are ready to feed them to your geckos. If you want them to grow more slowly, you can keep them in a cool basement for a day or two.

Do not offer tomato hornworms from outdoors to your leopard gecko.

Waxworms

These small, white, stocky caterpillars are the larvae of the greater wax moth, *Galleria mellonella*. They can grow to be about an inch (2.5 cm) long. These animals feed on beeswax in nature, so they are difficult to feed and gut-load. Keep them in their containers in the refrigerator to prolong their lives.

Waxworms are quite high in fats, so you should feed them only occasionally to your lizards. However, because of this high fat content, they are excellent for putting weight on geckos that are sickly or underfed and females that have just laid eggs.

Silkworms

Silkworms are caterpillars of the silk moth, *Bombyx mori*. Silkworms eat only mulberry leaves or a special commercial diet made mostly of mulberry leaves. Because of this specialized diet, they are difficult to raise. Mulberry leaves are high in calcium, which makes silkworms highly nutritious for leopard geckos. Silkworms get quite large, about 3 inches (around 7.5 cm) long, before turning into moths. Like hornworms, they should be kept in their containers with their food and fed as needed.

Silkworms feeding on mulberry leaves.

Bug Hunting

Some reptile keepers catch wild insects and other invertebrates to feed their pets. They might do this to save money, for fun, or to offer more variety to their herps. However, catching your own insects for food is not recommended. There are several risks involved with the practice:

- Pesticides
- Poisonous or dangerous insects
- Parasites

It is difficult to tell when an insect has been exposed to a pesticide or other toxic chemical. Flying insects can travel some distance from the site that was sprayed. Even in your own yard, you can't be sure what the neighbors treated their yards with, and therefore you can't be sure that the bugs in your yard didn't wander over from theirs with a toxic residue. Because leopard geckos are so small, it would not take much of a toxic chemical to harm them.

The same is true for poisonous insects. One bad bug could kill or harm a gecko. You can mitigate this risk somewhat by learning about the toxic insects in your area. Some common toxic insects in the United States include monarch butterflies, ladybugs, and lubber grasshoppers. As a general rule of thumb, if it is brightly colored or patterned, it is likely to be poisonous. Other invertebrates might be dangerous because they could injure the gecko by fighting back. Spiders and centipedes will bite back when attacked, and these might pose a danger to your gecko.

Lastly, wild invertebrates can carry parasites that can be transferred to a pet gecko. This poses a long-term risk to the health of the lizard. If you do feed wild-caught bugs to your gecko, you can lessen this risk by looking for evidence of worms in its droppings and taking your gecko to the vet for an exam annually, as well as at the first sign of weight loss or digestive issues.

There are so many varieties of domestically produced insects available now that catching wild insects seems too much of a risk for too little potential benefit.

Silkworms do not move a lot, so your leopard gecko may not be interested in them. You may need to either poke at the worms a little so they move or feed them to your gecko with forceps. Silk moths cannot fly. If some of your silkworms turn into moths before you feed them to your geckos, your geckos will be able to chase down and catch the moths.

Mice

Some keepers feed their adult leopard geckos small mice. Pink, or *pinky*, mice are newborns that have not yet begun to grow fur. Older mice that have just grown fur are often referred to as *fuzzies*.

There is no need to feed geckos mice, although they do pack quite a lot of nutrition into a single prey item and give a nutritional boost to females after laying eggs. Leopard geckos in nature seldom consume mammals. The high levels of protein and fat in mice may lead to health problems in your gecko if fed mice too frequently. Also, geckos that eat a lot of mice are more prone to obesity. A feeding of a single pink mouse is big meal for a leopard gecko. If you decide to feed your gecko mice, do so infrequently as treats.

GUT-LOADING

Crickets, roaches, and other insects are not very nutritious in and of themselves. They become nutritious only when they are fed a high-quality diet. This practice is called *gut-loading*. To ensure your leopard gecko maintains optimal health, gut-load all prey for at least twenty-four hours before feeding it to your gecko.

Crickets, roaches, and mealworms are easy to gut-load. Other prey should be fed an appropriate diet for their species. You can use a number of different items, either on their own or in combination, to gut-load crickets, roaches, and mealworms, including commercial cricket diets; powdered rabbit, guinea pig, or tortoise pellets (powdered in your blender); chicken mash; and cereal flakes for human babies. Many breeders also add calcium carbonate or a calcium/vitamin D3 supplement to the insect's diet.

Crickets are among the insects that must be gut-loaded before your gecko eats them.

For crickets and roaches, you can put the gut-load in a shallow dish, such as a jar lid, or just spread it on the floor of the enclosure. For mealworms, give them a deep enough layer of the gut-load to bury themselves in. Provide water as previously discussed.

SUPPLEMENTS

Even with gut-loading, leopard geckos need additional vitamin and mineral supplements for optimal health. Supplements fill any gaps in the geckos' nutrition. In the past, reptile keepers had to settle for using supplements intended for birds or mammals, but now there are a number of brands of reptile-specific supplements on the market. There are even supplements for specific species, although currently there are none that are specifically for leopard geckos. Use only supplements manufactured for use with reptiles.

With so many reptile vitamin/mineral supplements on the market, it can be hard to determine which is best for your leopard gecko. Each breeder, author, and expert has his or her own favorite. Truthfully, leopard geckos will do well on just about any of the commercially available brands. You may want to compare labels and look for the ones that contain the widest range of vitamins and minerals.

Calcium powder made for reptiles.

Another thing to look for is how the vitamin A is supplied. The best brands will supply vitamin A in the form of beta carotene. This helps prevent leopard geckos from getting too much vitamin A because their bodies convert the beta carotene into vitamin A as needed.

Powdered vitamin and mineral supplements are superior to liquid vitamins because powdered supplements stick easily to food whereas the liquid supplements do not. Also, do not put any supplements in your gecko's water. This enables bacteria to grow in the water more rapidly, and it is also difficult to know and control how much supplement your gecko is ingesting.

The most important requirement for leopard geckos is calcium. It is common practice to use both a calcium supplement and a multivitamin/mineral supplement to ensure that geckos get enough calcium.

Packaged Diets

There are a number of packaged diets for geckos, including frozen foods, pellets, pastes, and canned insects. The major problem with using them with leopard geckos is that they don't move. Movement is the primary stimulus for feeding. Without movement, most leopard geckos won't be interested.

If you want your gecko to eat a prepared diet, you will have to convince it. You can try putting the food in a bowl with some insects, like mealworms or waxworms. Eventually, you will eliminate the insects and hope the gecko has been conditioned to feed on just what's in the bowl. You can use forceps to wiggle the food. There are also bowls that vibrate, which makes the food move around. However, none of these methods is guaranteed to convince a leopard gecko that a pellet or a silkworm from a can is edible.

Calcium supplements often come with added vitamin D3, and this is fine to use with leopard geckos. In lizards that bask under real or artificial sunlight, supplementing vitamin D3 can result in giving the animal too much of this vitamin, but since leopard geckos are not baskers, there does not seem to be a risk of their getting too much vitamin D3. However, if you use a vitamin supplement that contains D3, it is important to use a calcium supplement that does not, and vice versa. By supplying vitamin D3 in only one of the supplements, you avoid the risk of giving too much.

To ensure that enough calcium is available to leopard geckos, the standard practice is to keep a small container, such as a jar lid, of powdered calcium supplement in the vivarium at all times. Your gecko will lick up the powder as it feels the need.

In addition to providing a dish of calcium, you can coat feeder insects with a vitamin/mineral mix (with or without added calcium). A mix that has performed well for many keepers consists of one part powdered reptile multivitamin/mineral supplement with two parts powdered calcium supplement. To coat insects with supplement, simply add a small amount of the powdered mix (one small pinch per insect) into a feeding jar. Put the insects into the jar, gently swirl the jar to lightly coat the insects, and then drop them into the vivarium feeding dish.

Immature leopard geckos can be supplemented at every feeding. Adults will fare well when supplemented only twice a week, although breeders often continue a high supplementation regime to ensure good egg production in females.

HOW AND WHEN TO FEED

The best way to feed leopard geckos is to offer feeder insects in shallow ceramic or glass dishes, plastic jars, or small pet dishes. This will prevent mealworms from escaping or burrowing into substrate and reduce the rate at which crickets disperse into the vivarium. It is important that the geckos eat the insects when they are still coated with the supplement. Even loose in the enclosure, dusted crickets will still have sufficient supplement stuck to them for a few hours.

To encourage rapid growth and good weight maintenance, many leopard gecko owners and breeders keep a dish filled with mealworms and powdered supplement in the enclosure at all times. Again, this diet can be supplemented once or twice a week with crickets or other food items.

Most keepers raise their leopard geckos primarily on crickets, which should not be offered ad libitum. Use only supplement-coated, appropriately sized crickets as previously recommended. Offer the crickets to juveniles every one to two days and to adult leopard geckos two to three times a week. Offer three to five properly sized crickets per feeding. The gecko should eat them all within fifteen minutes.

WATER

Offer clean water to your adult leopard geckos two to three times a week using a shallow container or plastic reptile dish. Use smaller containers, such as jar lids or petri dishes, to provide water to juveniles. Leopard geckos will drink water out of dishes in the same manner as a dog or cat would, but geckos cannot readily drink from tall containers in which the water is out of sight.

Change the water two to three times a week to prevent bacterial growth and fecal contamination. At least once a week, or whenever the water has been fouled, wash the water container with dish detergent and rinse thoroughly before adding new water. Once a month, disinfect water dishes by soaking them for thirty to sixty minutes in a 10 percent bleach solution. Rinse thoroughly before use. Having a spare water bowl or two can come in handy because you can just put the clean one in the cage while you disinfect the other one. This allows you to be prepared should your gecko foul its water bowl right before you leave for work or at another inconvenient time.

CHAPTER 5

HEALTH AND DISEASE

A healthy leopard gecko has clear eyes and no nasal secretions.

Leopard geckos are very hardy lizards, making necessary visits to the reptile veterinarian few and far between. With proper husbandry, you can avoid most medical issues in your gecko. However, you may encounter some problems, and these merit discussion.

POTENTIAL HEALTH ISSUES
HYPOCALCEMIA

Leopard geckos are somewhat more resistant to complications from low calcium levels (hypocalcemia) than most other commonly kept lizards. The signs include lethargy, weakness, painful movement, a softened or "rubbery" jaw, and swollen or distorted limbs. The lack of a calcium supplement with appropriate levels of vitamin D3 is the most common cause.

Because leopard geckos are primarily insectivores, it is imperative that keepers provide their geckos with insects that have been dusted with the appropriate supplements. While calcium supplements need to contain more calcium than phosphorus, reptile veterinarians are seeing the benefits of using calcium products that do not contain any phosphorus at all. Daily calcium dustings with a supplement that contains no vitamin D3 (usually pure calcium carbonate) for juveniles and every-other-day dustings for adults work well. Once a week, replace the calcium carbonate dusting with a calcium/D3 supplement. If

you notice signs of hypocalcemia, then increase the vitamin D3 dustings until you see an improvement. However, excessive vitamin D3 can cause soft tissue mineralization, so use good judgment and do not oversupplement.

Feeding pink mice once every two weeks also provides an excellent source of vitamins and minerals, including calcium and preformed vitamin D3. Avoid excessive feeding of pink mice because it can lead to obesity.

GASTROENTERITIS/DIARRHEA

The most obvious sign of gastrointestinal disease is weight loss combined with the presence of undigested cricket (or other prey) masses instead of the standard, relatively dry feces; the gecko may also regurgitate undigested prey. Other signs of gastrointestinal disorders include lethargy, anorexia, and unusually watery or bloody stools. A leopard gecko may also demonstrate a darkening of the iris (colored portion of the eye). Severely affected animals that have stopped eating and drinking are at great risk of dying.

A veterinarian can help determine the cause of the gastrointestinal crisis. Most gastroenteritis cases are due to bacterial infections; the veterinarian may need to perform a fecal culture to decide on an effective treatment.

It is important to have a fecal sample examined for intestinal parasites, such as trichomonads and coccidia. Trichomonads are flagellate protozoans that can be treated with daily doses of metronidazole over a course of three to five days at a dosage recommended by your veterinarian. Coccidia are another matter and much more difficult to eliminate.

Coccidia

The fact that geckos thrive in small containers makes them particularly susceptible to coccidia. Coccidia are tiny protozoan parasites that invade the intestinal lining in order to reproduce. The product of their reproduction is a tiny egg-like structure called an *oocyst*. The oocyst is the infective stage of the parasite and is passed with the fecal matter into the environment in the hopes that another host will become exposed to it.

A leopard gecko with coccidiosis in quarantine.

In a small, closed environment, geckos can repeatedly act as the host, with the numbers of coccidia increasing exponentially. When a parasite with a direct life cycle (meaning that no intermediate hosts are required) builds up like this, it is referred to as a *super-infection*. The irritation to the gastrointestinal tract leads to dehydration and anorexia and allows secondary bacteria to invade. Treatment consists of giving a sulfa-based drug such as sulfadimethoxine orally every twenty-four to forty-eight hours until resolved.

Medication alone, however, is insufficient. Fastidious cleaning is essential to fully eradicate coccidia. For an infected gecko, set up an extra cage and switch the gecko back and forth between cages once or twice a day. Use newspaper as a substrate for easy cleaning and eliminate all elaborate furnishings in the vivarium while the animal is being treated. Follow-up fecal exams are important to make sure that the coccidia have been eliminated. This is a very contagious parasite, passing easily from gecko to gecko, so you must strictly quarantine all new additions to a colony while evaluating them for parasites.

A particularly dire type of coccidian is *Cryptosporidium*, which causes a disease called *cryptosporidiosis*. Unfortunately, this has become a more widespread problem in the reptile hobby. Vomiting and rapid weight loss are the major signs.

Cryptosporidiosis is not curable. An infected leopard gecko can be stabilized for a time with medication and excellent nutrition, but the disease will ultimately kill the animal. A gecko suffering from this parasite should never be in contact with other reptiles because the disease easily spreads. Euthanizing an infected gecko is a sad but reasonable course of action.

Beware of Crypto

"Crypto"—short for *cryptosporidiosis*—is a dreaded disease that strikes fear in the hearts of every reptile keeper. It spreads easily to other animals and will eventually kill them. Even worse, humans can become infected, although it's treatable in humans. If you have to interact with a known or suspected carrier of crypto, take the utmost precautions to protect yourself and other humans and animals.

When caring for a gecko with cryptosporidiosis, practice extreme care to not introduce the parasite to any other reptiles you might have. Always feed the infected gecko and clean its enclosure after performing these tasks for the healthy animals. Wear gloves and wash your hands thoroughly *after* interacting with the infected animal. Consider wearing a smock or something similar that you can launder immediately after finishing your maintenance tasks. Humans can contract cryptosporidiosis, so take every possible precaution when working with animals suspected to carry the disease.

INFECTIONS OF THE DIGITS AND SKIN

Chronic shed problems can destroy the vascular pattern in a gecko's toes and result in the loss of digits. The traumatized and inflamed toes can become further insulted by exposure to substrate medium that is too moist or dirty. Not only will the toes become infected, but superficial skin infections, seen as discolored areas, may also occur.

The first step in resolving this problem is to address its cause. Replace soiled substrate media with newspaper or paper towels until the infection clears. You can treat mild superficial skin problems with

A young albino gecko with healthy skin and toes.

a neomycin and polymyxin B antibiotic cream, such as Polysporin or Neosporin, but severe cases will require veterinary intervention. Once the skin has healed, place the leopard gecko in an enclosure with clean, dry substrate.

MITES

Leopard geckos are not as susceptible to mites as many other lizards are, but they can get them. Mites are tiny arachnids related to ticks. They look like tiny specks of pepper, ranging in color from black or gray to reddish brown. The first sign of mites that a gecko keeper often notices is little flecks in the water bowl; these are mites that crawled into the bowl and drowned.

Mites feed on the blood of snakes and lizards, and the species found on reptiles do not infest mammals. Mites reproduce quickly. When they reach great numbers, they can severely impact the health of a leopard gecko. On top of draining the blood, there is some evidence that they can transmit disease between reptiles.

Mites pass easily from reptile to reptile. They can crawl some distance, so they can move between enclosures kept in the same room. They easily hitchhike on human hands, so handling an infested lizard is a good way to give mites to your other geckos. It is good practice to always wash your hands after handling snakes or lizards—for example, at a pet store or reptile show—before handling your own established and healthy reptiles.

Getting rid of mites is a frustrating chore. They will hide in substrate and cage décor. Prevention is best. Failing that, you will have to be diligent and meticulous in eradicating a mite infestation.

First, throw out any disposable substrate and décor—preferably in a sealed plastic bag in an outdoor garbage can. Then, carefully clean and disinfect any items that you can't throw out. Soak the items in a 10 percent bleach solution for at least 15 minutes and then rinse them several times until no bleach smell remains. Also clean the enclosure with the bleach solution, being careful to get the bleach into every nook and cranny. If any mites remain, they will breed, and the mite problem will just continue.

Mites on the gecko itself are trickier to remove. There are various over-the-counter mite sprays of varying effectiveness, or your veterinarian can prescribe a miticide. It's worth repeating that eradicating mites is difficult. They can fit into tiny spaces and are pretty hardy creatures. It's quite possible, even likely, that it will take you

As Bad as the Mites

Over the years, many substances, including organophosphates, human delousing agents, pyrethrins, and flea collars made for cats and dogs, have been used to get rid of mites, but none of these is recommended for use in reptiles. Their safety with reptiles is questionable at best, and there are reports of reptile deaths and injuries resulting from their usage.

more than one attempt to eliminate a mite infestation. Remember, prevention is a much better strategy than elimination.

STOMATITIS

Stomatitis—commonly called *mouthrot*—is often a primary mouth disease in reptiles. However, in leopard geckos, stomatitis is usually exhibited secondary to fighting. Symptoms include swelling, malocclusion (uneven upper and lower jaw), and a failure to eat well. On close inspection, you can see caseated (cheese-like) pus in the mouth, usually at the base of the teeth.

Clean the gecko's mouth with hydrogen peroxide or a diluted liquid antiseptic (Betadine), gently removing all loose tissue and pus. You can apply an extremely light layer of neomycin and polymyxin B antibiotic cream daily, but it can be toxic in excessive quantities. In all but the mildest cases, consult a veterinarian. Systemic antibiotics are generally required to resolve difficult cases.

Adequate heat inside the enclosure helps keep the leopard gecko healthy.

RESPIRATORY INFECTIONS

As is true with all reptiles, excessively cool temperatures (under 74°F [23°C]) for long periods of time will cause immune system suppression with subsequent respiratory infections. Symptoms may be subtle and include a partial opening of the mouth with labored expiration. Initially, a temperature change to a daytime high of 84–86°F (29–30°C) with a drop at night to no lower than 80°F (27°C) may be adequate for mild cases. If improvement is not seen quickly or symptoms worsen, consult a veterinarian.

EGG BINDING

Occasionally, a female leopard gecko will fail to pass one of the two eggs that typically forms. While you may be tempted to manipulate the egg out, it is difficult to do without irreversibly tearing the reproductive tract. Reproductive hormones, such as oxytocin, don't seem to resolve the problem. It is best to have the remaining egg removed surgically by a veterinarian.

Egg binding may be due in part to hypocalcemia; calcium is essential to the contraction of the reproductive smooth muscle. Feed gravid (pregnant) females calcium supplements daily.

SHEDDING PROBLEMS

Like other reptiles, leopard geckos periodically shed their entire epithelial skin (outer layer of the skin). The process of shedding the skin is called *ecdysis*. Between shed cycles, when leopard geckos replace the superficial layers of their skin, their skin is in a resting stage that ends when the cells that generate the new skin begin to divide. This starts the actual shed cycle and, as can be expected, the process affects the geckos' coloration.

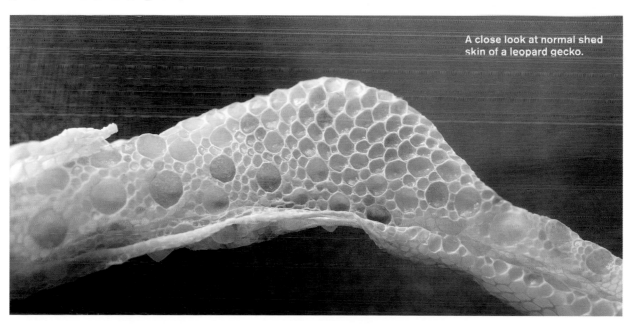

A close look at normal shed skin of a leopard gecko.

Skin: It's What's for Dinner

It might sound disgusting, but leopard geckos usually eat their shed skin. Why they do this is not known for sure, but several theories exist. One theory is that they are reclaiming lost minerals and protein; another is that they make it harder for predators to track their scent by eating the skin. Whatever the reason, it's totally natural and nothing to be alarmed about.

As the shed cycle begins, a leopard gecko's skin becomes progressively duller until the underlying new skin is fully formed and the superficial old skin begins to separate from it. At this point, the gecko looks like it is covered with a thin, papery membrane. The old skin then starts detaching itself in sheetlike sections, much like a person's skin peels after a sunburn. Like many types of gecko, leopard geckos seize the peeling sections in their mouths and consume them, possibly to ingest certain nutrients contained in the skin. In the wild, eating the skin probably reduces the scent markers that attract potential predators, such as snakes and predatory mammals. Leopard geckos' coloration is brightest right after they have shed.

A leopard gecko that fails to shed looks dull and pale, and the old skin adhering to the body, eyelids, and extremities is easy to see. The gecko also tends to be listless. Failure to shed indicates a serious problem and can result in death if not quickly addressed. The digits appear to be the most susceptible to vascular damage, and retained sheds will lead to their sloughing.

Low temperatures, a lack or overabundance of vitamin A, weakness caused by injury, bacterial infections, parasites, metabolic bone disease, and low relative humidity are all factors that contribute to shedding problems. Low humidity is the most common cause.

Provide proper diet supplementation to eliminate any dietary causes, and provide a humidified shelter to ensure that adequate humidity is available to your leopard gecko. By closely observing your leopard gecko, including its feces, level of activity, and weight loss or gain, you will be able to determine whether it has a bacterial or parasitic disease. A qualified veterinarian should be consulted for proper diagnosis and treatment. If ignored, failure to shed can result in eye problems, loss or infection of the digits, and, in extreme cases, death.

You can use a cotton swab dipped in hydrogen peroxide to soften and gently remove the adherent skin, but be careful not to get peroxide into the gecko's eyes. If humidity is the issue, you can put the gecko in a small container with some moist paper towels on the bottom. Make sure that the container has adequate air holes, but it should not be overly ventilated. You want the lizard to be in a humid environment. After about an hour, its dead skin should come off easily. The long-term solution is to make adjustments to ensure adequate humidity in the gecko's enclosure.

For skin that is still firmly attached, moisturize it with an ophthalmic (eye) lubricant ointment. Once softened, you can gently—but never forcefully—remove the pieces of skin.

Shedding problems are best prevented by the use of a moist hide box. For example, you can construct a mini humidity chamber from a clean plastic food-storage container with an entry and exit hole cut into it. Fill the inside of the chamber with vermiculite or sphagnum moss. Humidity chambers also serve as sites for females to lay their eggs.

TAIL LOSS

Like most geckos, a leopard gecko will drop its tail if threatened or grabbed by the tail. This ability is called *caudal autotomy*. Following autotomy, the original tail will twitch on the ground. In the wild, the squirming tail holds the attention of a predator and provides a snack while the leopard gecko escapes.

The caudal (tail) vertebrae of leopard geckos have connective-tissue fracture points that allow the tail or a section of the tail to autotomize easily. This process is accompanied by rapid

A leopard gecko in the process of regrowing its tail.

A high-yellow leopard gecko with a regenerated tail.

vasoconstriction, which minimizes blood loss. Although leopard geckos can grow new tails, what replaces the original tail section is a bulbous, unringed structure that is no longer supported by bony vertebrae but instead by a cartilaginous rod. The regrown tail is not as aesthetically pleasing as the original. It tends to be shorter, and it acquires proportions that make it resemble the head. If attacked again, a leopard gecko can drop the entire regrown section.

Tail loss in a leopard gecko is caused not only by predator attacks but also by intraspecies aggression (being attacked by a member of its own species). Male leopard geckos may attack each other; babies may drop their tails during feeding frenzies or fights; and aggressive females or sexually overzealous males may cause tail loss. When a leopard gecko drops its tail, it loses a significant amount of fat reserve and is more vulnerable to stress. Remove the leopard gecko and keep it by itself in a separate enclosure until its tail has regenerated. Keep the tailless animal warm, fed, and watered regularly. It is rare for the wound where the tail was to become infected, but it is possible. Examine the conditions that caused the tail loss and take the necessary steps to prevent it from reoccurring.

FINDING A REPTILE VETERINARIAN

There may be times when your leopard gecko needs medical care, and you are better off taking your pet to a reptile veterinarian rather than to a vet who deals primarily with dogs and cats. Fortunately, as reptile keeping has grown in popularity, veterinarians who treat reptiles have become easier to find.

You can usually find a veterinarian with reptile experience via an online search of the term "reptile veterinarian" or "exotic animal veterinarian." You might also consult local herpetological societies (most states and some counties and towns have them), animal shelters, or pet stores for recommendations. The Association of Reptilian and Amphibian Veterinarians also maintains a database of reptile vets on their website, www.arava.org.

It is better to find a reptile veterinarian before an emergency. When there's an emergency, knowing who to call and where to go will save you time and stress. The best practice is to start a relationship with a reptile vet when your gecko is still healthy. Taking your new gecko in for a general checkup allows you to verify that your gecko is healthy and to get to know the vet. You will be able to find out essential information about the vet's practice, such as regular hours, emergency policies, and any additional services, such as if the vet's office will board your gecko when you go on vacation. Building a good relationship with a reptile veterinarian is more than worth the time and money you will spend.

CHAPTER 6

BREEDING LEOPARD GECKOS

A leopard gecko hatches.

L eopard geckos are possibly the easiest of all lizards currently available in herpetoculture to breed. In fact, they will often breed even if you make no special efforts to help the process along.

WHY BREED LEOPARD GECKOS?

There is no shortage of leopard geckos on the market. There are several large-scale commercial breeders of leopard geckos, many small-scale commercial breeders, and a great number of hobbyist breeders in existence. So, why breed your leopard geckos?

Breeding leopard geckos is fun. Many keepers find it interesting to participate in the process of mating, egg laying, hatching, and raising offspring. Breeding his or her first geckos gives an enthusiast a sense of accomplishment. Even with the vast numbers of leopard geckos being bred, new color and pattern variations are created all the time; some breeders work with leopard geckos specifically to develop these varieties. Additionally, if you ever want to breed rarer, more expensive, or more delicate lizard species, breeding leopard geckos is a great way to gain experience with breeding lizards.

Money is not a good reason to breed leopard geckos. It's quite possible to have a profitable business breeding leopard geckos. However, it will not be easy, nor will your income be guaranteed. There are so many sources for leopard geckos these days that it is difficult to break into the marketplace. If you want to breed your leopard geckos, it's important to know that your chances of getting rich off the enterprise are close to nonexistent.

WHEN TO BREED

As with many reptiles, size is more important than age as the primary criterion for determining a leopard gecko's sexual maturity. Leopard geckos generally reach sexual maturity at a weight of around 1.25 ounces (35 grams). Many breeders grow their animals to about 1.5 ounces (40 grams) before they breed them. Depending on the temperature at which they are raised, leopard geckos reach maturity between ten and twenty-four months. Most animals in captivity will breed for the first time between fourteen and eighteen months of age.

REQUIREMENTS FOR SUCCESSFUL BREEDING

The first condition for successful breeding is to have at least one male leopard gecko and one or more females. The second condition is to have healthy leopard geckos. Finally, the leopard geckos should not be too old. The best breeders are two to three years old. Females older than six years can breed, but they produce fewer eggs. Females older than nine years will produce few, if any, eggs. Males can breed successfully at older ages, although the number of offspring they sire may decline when they reach an advanced age.

PREBREEDING CONDITIONING

As mentioned, all leopard geckos used for breeding should be in prime condition and at healthy body weights. Many owners do not precondition their animals in any special manner prior to breeding. Others expose their animals to a prebreeding conditioning period consisting of shorter photoperiods (less than twelve hours of daylight per twenty-four hours) and cooler temperatures (as low as 65°F [around 18°C]

The albino trait, shown here, was first recorded by breeders in 1996.

at night and 72–76°F [around 22–24°C] during the day) for four to eight weeks prior to breeding attempts. Because both cooler temperature and reduced daylight are natural features of winters in most countries, implementing this kind of conditioning requires little effort. Breeders have success with both cooling their geckos and not cooling them; if you have poor results with the cooling regimen, try again with no preconditioning.

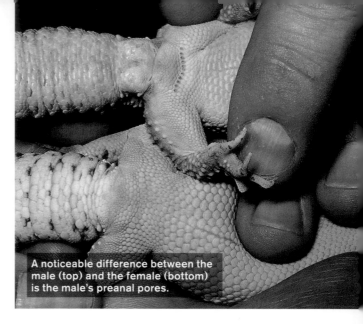

A noticeable difference between the male (top) and the female (bottom) is the male's preanal pores.

Cool It!

If you decide to cool your geckos, it is best to cool them gradually. Drop the temperature at the hottest spot in the cage a few degrees each day until you reach daytime temperatures of 72–76°F (around 22–24°C). The gradual cooling should take about two weeks. Having your heating device connected to a rheostat will make this process easier.

Breeding Season

In captivity, leopard geckos usually breed during a season that extends from January to September. Some captive leopard geckos begin breeding late in the season, and they breed up to and including the month of October. Under controlled conditions, leopard geckos can be made to breed at any time of the year.

BREEDING METHODS
GROUP BREEDING

Most owners use a group breeding method, housing one male with up to twenty females. This is sometimes called the *harem method* or a *harem setup*. From a production point of view, this method has a clear economic advantage because you are not wasting resources feeding, raising, and housing large numbers of males. Under these conditions, you can keep males with females year round, although some breeders claim better success when they remove the males during the few months when leopard geckos are not breeding.

For those interested in commercial-scale leopard gecko breeding, the group breeding method is the most effective. To maximize production, keep careful records on the production levels of established groups. Poor reproductive performance requires careful evaluation of breeding stock, health status, and husbandry methods. To increase the probability of reproductive success, it is a good idea to alternate males in breeding groups at least once. Not all males are good breeders.

Carefully monitor all of your animals. Some females may not compete as well as others for food and may show signs of gradual weight loss. Evidence of fighting and the occasional loss of a tail may require you to remove one or more animals temporarily from a particular group.

Quarantine all new stock individually in separate areas from established stock. Always wash your hands after handling or

A beautiful yellow-orange morph.

maintaining new stock. The senior author has seen several breeders and hobbyists devastated when coccidiosis infected their entire colonies.

SINGLE ANIMAL INTRODUCTION

Breeders interested in carefully controlled pairings to develop new morphs may keep their leopard geckos singly and introduce females to stud males during the breeding season. Females with developing eggs visible through the abdominal wall tend to be more receptive to male breeding attempts. This method allows for controlled breeding that you can track and also tends to be quite effective. A male kept singly will often readily breed when a female is suddenly introduced to its

Another example of Bill Brant's yellow-orange line.

territory. Another advantage to this method is that when females are maintained singly, except for short reproductive encounters, they experience less stress because males do not continually pester them.

EGG LAYING AND INCUBATION

Leopard geckos typically produce multiple clutches of two eggs during the breeding season. Occasionally, single-egg hatches are laid, usually from very young or older females. As a rule, young geckos produce one to three clutches during their first year; as they mature, they will produce up to five clutches of eggs in a year. Breeders who have made concerted efforts to maintain their animals under optimal conditions have reported animals laying up to eight clutches of fertile eggs a year. After several years of peak breeding, older leopard geckos tend to gradually produce fewer eggs and fertility is decreased. Eventually, old leopard geckos stop breeding altogether.

EGG LAYING

As female leopard geckos get closer to depositing eggs, the developing eggs within the female become more clearly defined and cause slight bulging at the sides of the abdomen. Breeders use two methods for collecting eggs: leaving their setup as it is or adding a laying chamber (often called a *nest box* or *laying box*).

If you opt to leave the setup as is, mist the inside of your gecko's shelter daily so that the ground medium is slightly damp. Most female geckos will find the moist shelter to be an attractive nest site, although it's always possible for a female to reject a nest site. Check the shelter for eggs at least daily. Also, you will need to check around the enclosure in case the female rejected the shelter and laid her eggs elsewhere. If that happens, you have to find the eggs before they dry out.

Gecko Eggs

Freshly laid leopard gecko eggs tend to be somewhat soft and sticky. Fertile eggs quickly firm up and are covered with a thick, leathery, chalk-white membrane while infertile eggs often remain thin and soft and fail to become turgid.

Some breeders prefer to construct an egg-laying chamber made from a plastic container, such as a food-storage container with its lid on, half-filled with vermiculite or sand. Add water to make the vermiculite moist but not soggy. A good way to judge is to take a bit in your hand and squeeze. You'll be able to squeeze a few drops, not a stream, of water out.

The covered container must be large enough for the female to enter. You will need to cut a hole in the side for her to enter just above the layer of moistened medium. If there are any sharp edges or points, rub them smooth with sandpaper.

Often, but not always, a female will select this egg-laying chamber as her laying site. The advantage of this method is that if a female utilizes the chamber, the eggs are not likely to desiccate. It can also help save you time because you will not have to look throughout the entire enclosure for the eggs.

The high yellow is a very popular morph.

White leopard geckos are also marketed as "snow" leopard geckos.

INCUBATION OF EGGS

For proper egg incubation, the leopard gecko eggs must absorb moisture primarily from the high relative humidity of the atmosphere. High relative humidity will cause them to gain weight, but a too-moist incubating medium can result in too much internal water pressure within the eggs. When this happens to an egg, its shell appears stretched and semitransparent. Too much moisture also creates a greater possibility that the eggs will be attacked by fungus.

One common way to incubate eggs is to use a plastic shoebox or sweater-sized plastic storage box as an incubation box. You can use 1–1.5 inches (3–4 cm) of barely moistened coarse vermiculite or a 50/50 vermiculite/perlite mix added as an incubating medium. There are also reptile incubation media on the market; these offer great incubation results. If you want to use one of these products, you will likely need to order it online or go to a reptile show because you will probably not find it in a pet-supply store.

Leopard gecko eggs incubating in vermiculite.

To obtain the proper moisture level, mix six parts incubating medium with four parts water by weight. However, many breeders simply add water to the medium and mix it by hand until it feels damp but not wet. As with the medium in the nest box, you should be able to squeeze out only a few drops of water rather than a stream or steady dripping.

Place the eggs on their sides and bury them halfway within the medium. Try not to turn the eggs over when moving them from the nest box to the incubation box. The top side of the egg as it has been laid should remain the top side; otherwise, there is a chance of killing the embryo inside.

You can place a small container, such as a jar lid, of water on top of the medium to maintain high relative air humidity. Place the lid on the storage box. Most lids are loose enough to allow some airflow, but if you do not plan on regularly opening the box to check the eggs, drill tiny holes in the upper part of each side of the box for ventilation.

Incubators

Other methods for incubation include the use of a reptile egg incubator, a small poultry incubator (such as a Hova-Bator), or a homemade incubator with a submersible aquarium heater. If using a reptile or poultry egg incubator, follow the manufacturer's instructions.

To construct a homemade incubator, simply purchase a submersible aquarium heater (75–100 watts is suitable for smaller incubators). Place it at the bottom of an aquarium (at least a standard 20-gallon [75-liter] tank is recommended) or large Styrofoam container, such as those used to ship fish to pet stores. Pet stores will often give these away if you ask.

Add water to a height of .5–2 inches (1–5 cm) above the heater. Build a platform above the water level to set your egg-incubating containers on. There are various methods of doing this. Some people simply set a section of thick, wire-welded fencing across a couple of bricks, while others construct a plexiglass structure that can easily be taken in and out of the aquarium. The platform can be anything that is taller than the depth of the water and big enough to fit the incubation

The Hova-Bator is a popular incubator among leopard gecko breeders.

The Hova-Bator features an adjustable thermostat and thermometer and viewing windows.

box on. You will eventually place the incubation box, with eggs, on the platform. Finally, construct a tight-fitting polystyrene foam lid to cover the top of the aquarium incubator. A Styrofoam fish-shipping box normally will come with a lid.

The principle for this type of incubator is simple: a submersible heater in a low level of water in the aquarium heats up the air above the water to the desired temperature. You just have to develop a method of suspending the egg containers inside the heated air, and that's where the platform comes in.

The key to accurately determining the temperature is proper calibration of the submersible heater. To do this, you must first calibrate it with an empty container inside the incubator because you don't want to overheat the eggs.

Calibrating Incubators

Whether you are using a poultry incubator or a homemade incubator, you must calibrate the thermostat to the desired temperature. The key is using a good thermometer inside the container. Electronic digital thermometers with thermal sensors (for outside temperature) are available in electronics-supply stores and through reptile-supply companies. They are relatively inexpensive, depending on their features. The most expensive will give a daily minimum and maximum temperature reading. Some even have an alarm system that beeps to warn you when the temperature goes above or below a given setting.

Calibrating an incubator can take quite a bit of time, so do it before your female lays eggs. Properly calibrating the incubator is critical to your hatching success.

Keep the digital thermometer outside the incubator where you can easily read it and then place the sensor inside the incubating container and switch to the "out" reading. This will allow for a continuous readout of the temperature. By contrast, a standard thermometer will require you to open the container to get an accurate reading. As a backup, use an inexpensive, standard thermometer to occasionally verify the readings. Whatever thermometer you are using, calibration will require small adjustments to the thermostatic control of the incubator.

> **Calibration Tip**
>
> Once set, let the incubator run awhile before proceeding with the next adjustment. To be safe, allow up to an hour for the temperature to settle to the new thermostat adjustment.

An on-off thermostat is the least expensive and most widely used type of thermostat, and it will help keep the temperature steady in the incubator. With this type of thermostat, if the recorded temperature goes above or below the set temperature, the heating unit turns off automatically. This provides a good backup to the aquarium heater. The more advanced pulse-proportional type of thermostat is available mainly through herpetological supply companies. It allows you to easily and very precisely set and maintain desired incubator temperatures. The temperature readings are taken steadily, and you control the heating device by an electronic rheostat, which regulates the current of the unit to produce the desired level of heat.

Incubation Temperatures

Studies by Brian Viets, PhD, and others have confirmed that leopard gecko sex is determined by temperature within the first two weeks of incubation. If the eggs are incubated at a temperature of 79°F

A lavender top-banded gecko.

An example of a ghost leopard gecko.

(26°C), most of the offspring will be female. At temperatures of 85–87°F (29–31°C), there will be a more or less equal ratio of males and females. At 90°F (32°C), the great majority of the hatchlings will be males.

Herpetoculturists, depending on their goals, should determine the preferred incubation temperature(s) for their specific purposes. To obtain males, incubate eggs at 89–90°F (around 32°C) for the first three to four weeks and then incubate them at cooler temperatures—80–85°F (27–29°C)—to reduce any risk of mortality from incubating the eggs too close to their warmer temperature limits (about 95°F [35°C]). When the goal is large-scale breeding for the pet trade, breeding for females is more desirable because they can be kept together in groups.

Check the incubating eggs, the incubating medium, and any water containers on a regular basis. Depending on incubation temperatures, leopard gecko eggs will hatch in six to fifteen weeks.

RAISING THE HATCHLINGS

It is ideal to house juvenile leopard geckos individually in plastic shoeboxes, each with a small shelter and a shallow water dish. If you need to house your hatchlings in groups, separate them by size to prevent feeding competition. As a rule, larger or more dominant leopard geckos chase prey more vigorously and intimidate smaller leopard geckos. The result in a mixed colony of babies is that some grow much faster

A hatchling leopard gecko with high-contrast bands.

and therefore compete more effectively for available food items. Small animals may remain small and eventually start to decline. Keeping babies in large containers, offering plenty of food, and segregating by size will help prevent these kinds of problems.

During the first week following hatching, baby leopard geckos live off of their yolk reserves. They do not begin feeding until after their first shed, which should occur within this first week. Feed hatchlings and juveniles two- to three-week-old vitamin/mineral-supplemented crickets every one to two days. You can also offer half-grown mealworms with calcium powder in feeding dishes that prevent the mealworms from escaping. A shallow water dish should be available at all times. In addition, lightly mist the inside of shelters two to three times a week to increase relative air humidity and to facilitate shedding.

COMMERCIAL BREEDING

All areas of agricultural production require careful research and evaluation. You need to ask yourself what it is you want to do: produce leopard geckos commercially on a large scale or produce the more valuable

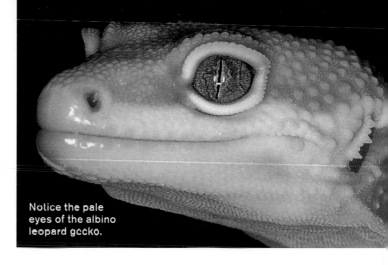

Notice the pale eyes of the albino leopard gecko.

morphs on a smaller scale. Again, you can make a comparison with goldfish and koi carp production. The focus of the endeavor on the specialist level is aesthetic. It caters to how combinations of color and pattern affect the human mind. As with goldfish, there is a very large commercial market that is an outlet for mass-produced forms.

It is difficult to ascertain the outcome of breeding by observing the hatchlings. You might have a high yellow, jungle, or striped hatchling, but you cannot accurately predict the qualities of the adult. For the morphs to become well established and to maintain the vigor of the species, culling, outbreeding, and introducing new blood are important. While morphs that have large commercial appeal depend on selection by the general buying public, the values of new and expensive morphs are determined by the breeder/specialist market.

My Leopard Geckos Won't Breed!

Surprisingly, questions relating to the failure of leopard geckos to breed are not uncommon. There are many reasons why leopard geckos will not breed, usually associated with husbandry, health, or incompatibility. The following is an overview of reasons why leopard geckos will not breed.

- You don't have a sexual pair. Finding out that "Henry" is, in fact, "Henrietta" is not uncommon among first-time owners of these lizards. So, a first step is to make sure that you have actually put a pair together. Check for preanal pores. If you can't determine the sex, consult your local reptile store or visit your veterinarian.
- You are keeping the lizards at suboptimal temperatures. Although cooling does not appear to be necessary for leopard geckos to successfully breed, providing adequate heat is a must.
- Your lizards are ill. Various diseases will debilitate leopard geckos, preventing them from accumulating sufficient fat and calcium reserves for egg production. Weak, thin females may have problems laying eggs. High levels of parasites can prevent successful fertilization.
- The geckos are either too small and sexually immature, or they are too old and females are post-reproductive.

Color and Pattern Variations

by Ron Tremper

It is safe to say that the leopard gecko is the most widely bred terrarium reptile in the world, so it is no surprise that its genetic possibilities would emerge and develop through the growing field of herpetoculture. There are now more *morphs*—variations of color and/or pattern produced by breeders—of leopard geckos than of any other reptile, with the likely exception of the ball python. As of 2017, 111 morphs were recognized by the Leopard Gecko Wiki site (www.leopardgeckowiki.com), and more will surely be developed and discovered. Breeders also combine different morphs, so an individual leopard gecko could be hypomelanistic (lacking dark coloration) and striped, for example.

Here I will discuss some of the morphs, but providing a full encyclopedia of morphs is beyond the scope of the book. Some terms are useful to define here. A *gene* is the molecular code for a certain trait, such as albinism. Genes occur in pairs; a leopard gecko gets one of the pair from its mother and the other from its father. A *genotype* is the genetics of an organism, and the *phenotype* is the outward appearance. The genotype and phenotype can be different, as in the case of recessive genes. A recessive gene does not show in the phenotype unless the organism has two copies, one from each parent; for example, albinism is recessive. A dominant gene will show in the phenotype even though the lizard carries only one copy of it. There are some genes that are partially dominant or that give a certain appearance if there is one copy and a different appearance if there are two copies. When there are two copies of the same gene, the lizard is *homozygous* for that gene. If the copies are different—for example, one gene for albinism and one for normal appearance—the lizard is *heterozygous* for that trait.

As of 1990, the only variation available in the pet trade was the high yellow morph. This morph was merely a normal patterned gecko with an intense yellow or gold color predominating the body, sometimes with small amounts of orange around the top of the tail base.

In 1978, I acquired my first adult geckos. By 1998, these geckos had been bred to the twentieth generation without any additional stocks being added. These geckos were *line bred*, which is to say that they were of one large, related family group or lineage. Such breeding practices eventually express any recessive or hidden traits in a given population.

A melanistic banded leopard gecko.

It was not until 1991 that a baby randomly hatched with two black longitudinal body stripes that ran from the head to the base of the tail. This partial striped female was then bred back to its father, resulting in the first striped and first jungle-phase geckos. These offspring were the first geckos I had ever seen with a tail pattern other than the normal four or five rings. They had dorsally isolated tail blotches of white, and one had a complete straight-edged white stripe to the tip of the tail.

Many variations quickly emerged through selective breeding, and the term *designer leopard gecko* was born.

PATTERN

From the beginning, I chose to select three recessive traits, two of which involved pattern, in my founding stocks of designer geckos: reduced numbers of dark head spots, bright body colors of yellow or orange, and aberrant patterns. Basically, I found that the variations discovered in all geckos were the results of simple recessive gene pairings. As a hobbyist, you will get offspring that resemble the parents if both parents are mutations themselves. However, if you breed a wild-caught leopard gecko to any known mutation, you will mask the mutation if the wild-type parent is carrying no recessive traits.

Normal: A normal pattern gecko (typical wild morph, representative of those found in the wild) has two dark transverse body bands and three to four dark tail rings with numerous dark body and head spots mixed with a light cream or tan color. The wild-type pattern is fully evident at hatching and becomes obscured with age. The dark bands and rings may appear as shades of purple or violet at sexual maturity. The light cream or tan color is not well defined in any set pattern.

Jungle: The jungle phase gecko is a highly variable, aberrant gecko with irregular, asymmetrical, and dark body blotches and a non-ringed tail. The jungle phase has dark, bold spots on the limbs; it is from this pattern mutation that the first fully striped geckos came. The jungle-phase trait is dominant over the striped trait.

A jungle-phase female produced in 1994 was hatched with a uniquely shaped head and a blunt tail about two-thirds the length of a normal tail. The animal was sterile. This condition is probably genetically linked to her peculiar body shape.

Striped: The striped gecko is an aberrant gecko with a light-colored longitudinal dorsal stripe. The stripe joins with the white neck ring and runs to the base of the tail or tail tip.

This morph speaks for itself and is a very common mutation in many species of reptile, particularly snakes. In a true "striper," the vertebral light-colored stripe joins completely with the white neck ring; otherwise, it is considered a partial-stripe morph. The stripe phase never has a normally ringed tail pattern. The tail might be either entirely or partially striped or blotched.

Reverse stripe: This is an aberrant gecko with a dark-colored longitudinal dorsal stripe that joins with the white neck ring and may be broken at the tail base. The tail is predominately white with dark dorsal blotches or striping.

As the name implies, this pattern morph displays a complete reversal of the body and tail colors. It was first developed in 1997.

Patternless: This aberrant gecko lacks all dark pigment markings and patterns and has normal-colored eyes. In 1991, a California breeder announced a strange gecko he had produced from seemingly normal-appearing parents, giving rise to the so-called leucistic morph that has become so popular. This gecko hatches out with large brown or tan blotches over a very pale or cream-colored body. With growth, as in all leopard geckos, the blotches are lost through the movement of pigment cells in the skin. The result is a striking gecko with a light yellow body and head and tail coloring that is lighter than the cream color it hatched with.

All leopard geckos can change color to some extent, but when you remove the darker pigments, these color changes are much more evident. A top-quality leucistic can look like a bronze-colored lizard one moment and an exquisite light-colored gem the next. Some examples of this form, however, stay dark brown as adults. Other variations of patternless geckos are those missing all dark body spots and bands but are from a different gene than the leucistic.

A baby albino leopard gecko.

COLOR

Color variation is one of the most important aspects of the popularity of designer and mutation leopard geckos. The bright blue or turquoise color seen on the top of the head and between the eyes of hatchling geckos is normal and fades, and then disappears, with age.

Normal: This gecko has black, brown, shades of purple, and cream coloration. The wild-caught or normal-phase geckos are a mixture of subdued black, brown, and shades of purple, with a light cream or tan coloration that lacks intensity. Wild populations contain numerous recessive genes that herpetoculturists are expressing as new phenotypes (the observable physical characteristics) each year.

High yellow: This type of gecko has an extremely bright yellow or gold background coloration with any pattern phase. Coined names, such as *golden* and *hyperxanthic*, refer to one and the same morph but may represent different lines of breeding. The high yellow morph is extremely beautiful when the color is seen on animals that lack most of the small dark body and head spots. The color can appear on all of the known pattern variations.

High yellows can be determined at hatching by examining the hind legs. If the femur (the area from the body to the knee joint) is entirely yellow—missing the traditional dark streak on top of the leg—in color, then the newborn will become a high yellow.

Orange/tangerine: This gecko has an orange pigment anterior to the tail base. Orange and tangerine represent the same variation but are a lineage developed by different breeders through selective efforts. Actually, they are offshoots of the same gene.

Several private colonies were linebred for numerous years to obtain this orange coloration anterior to the tail base. Orange, to varying degrees, was common on leopard gecko tails, but it was not until 1996 that breeders succeeded in getting any significant amounts of orange on the body in adults.

Carrot-tail geckos have a lot of bright orange color on the tail. To be a true carrot-tail, the gecko must have a tail that is at least 15 percent orange. Some particularly stunning leopard geckos have been created by crossing carrot-tails with tangerines and hypomelanistic animals in various combinations.

White: In adults, black and white colors predominate. The hypomelanistic (lacking melanin), or snow, geckos fall into this class of gecko color variation. Such animals are black and white at hatching and remain that way as adults. The amount of black pigment can vary due to selective breeding, and white geckos may be represented by any pattern morph.

The Mack super snow is one type of white leopard gecko developed by commercial breeder John Mack. It has a solid white body with purple to black markings. The eye is black with no pupil readily visible.

Lavender: This coloration is indicated when adults have shades of purple predominately on the body and tail with a cream or yellow background. The lavenders are a natural result of the changes that occur in all dark—almost black—birth bands on the body and tail regions. Pigment cells migrate as the gecko grows, and the result can be large vivid purplish blotches on a light cream or high yellow background. At hatching, lavender hatchlings resemble normal or banded high yellow phase.

Ghost: A ghost gecko is of any pattern phase with extremely faded colors and greatly reduced dark pigmentation. Animals with this color only express it after they reach the size of 5–6 inches (13–15 cm) total length. They start out looking like dark colored hatchlings, but their color lightens and fades with each passing month. This is a very pale, healthy gecko morph with genetically caused fading, which is not to be confused with a female at the end of the egg-laying season whose natural colors fade due to nutritional depletion.

Melanistic: The melanistic gecko is predominately black with any pattern phase. Several breeders are developing black phase geckos. The young have white lips and all-black hind limbs at birth, and the spaces between the dominant body markings turn a dark yellow as the geckos mature. Two dark morphs, the black velvet and black pearl, are being developed by breeders and are the closest to an all-black leopard gecko that has been seen thus far.

Amelanistic: This is an albino gecko that genetically lacks melanin. It can be of any pattern phase. For decades, herpetoculturists dreamed of the world's first commercially available albino leopard gecko. In September 1996, the first albino to hatch in captivity occurred randomly through the incidental crossing of two heterozygous (normal-looking), wild-imported geckos by a California breeder. This animal was a female banded morph and shared an isolated egg cup with her heterozygous brother. Captive breeding efforts of this unique and rare mutation continued, and albinos are now readily available in the hobbyist trade.

Additionally, and quite amazingly, a male albino occurred randomly in 1998 from a Nevada breeder. The male's parents can be traced back to that very same group of 1996 wild-imported adults. There is a third line of albinos available as well. The three lines are the result of three different mutations.

Leucistic: The leucistic is a white gecko of any pattern phase that has black or blue eyes. A true leucistic gecko is one that has totally white pigment over all of its skin as an adult. It differs from the patternless animals in that the surface of the skin is dominated by iridophores (iridophores contribute color through their physical properties, causing the diffraction of light to reflect).

IN CONCLUSION

The art of herpetoculture has a tremendous palette for anyone to embrace. The selective breeding of leopard geckos is a new frontier awaiting the beginner as well as the advanced breeder. The koi carp of lizards has arrived.

SELECTING BREEDER STOCK

As mentioned earlier, hatchling leopard geckos do not fully reflect what the adults will become. The advantage to starting off with hatchlings is that you can purchase them for substantially less than subadults, and you also will know the age of your stock. It is a gamble because the animals may not end up exactly like what you had in mind—but they could be even nicer than you expected.

Subadults or young adults are generally more expensive, but they give you a much better idea of what your adults will look like. You also won't have to wait so long before they start producing, potentially returning your initial investment within the first year. Finally, you will still know the age of the animals you are buying. A generally risky proposition is buying large adults or retired breeders. The advantage is that you will know exactly what the animals look like, but the disadvantage is that they may be old and have low productivity.

THE VALUE OF MALES

For introducing genetic mutations in captive breeding projects, male leopard geckos are valuable in the same way as award-winning stallions or bulls. Assume, for example, that you have a colony of leopard geckos and that you want to commercially breed the newest amelanistic (albino) line. If you buy a single

hatchling male and introduce it to fifty normal females, within fourteen months you could produce five hundred animals heterozygous for albinism. Another twenty-four months, and the mature heterozygous offspring would be able to produce at least a thousand albinos (four years, or two generations, is about the average length of time that a new leopard gecko mutation can maintain a high value before prices decline).

In contrast, if you purchased a single female, you would have between ten and twelve heterozygous hatchlings with the first breeding, and around twenty-five albino hatchlings in another twenty-four months. The value of males for introducing new genetic material to a colony is evident. Only a few males are needed for large-scale production, and breeders often choose to limit the number of males produced by temperature, manipulating the sex determination of captive-bred offspring. In the economic scheme of things, ordinary male leopard geckos are no more valuable, and possibly less valuable, than females. However, outstanding males are worth their weight in gold.

KEEPING RECORDS

Successful breeders typically keep records. They record the origins of their adult animals, the dates they were obtained, and their ages. They record the number of eggs laid and the laying dates are for individual females or for each breeding container. Good breeders also record the parentage of egg clutches and offspring. These records allow breeders to determine when annual egg production is declining and whether they need to replace breeder stock for optimal reproduction. Records also allow breeders to trace the origins of specific lines and new mutations that have popped up in their colonies and to selectively breed lines in a controlled manner. Computers are invaluable for record keeping; there are even programs specifically designed for herpetoculture records.

MANAGING BREEDING COLONIES

Leopard gecko colonies take up space and require good management for optimal production. Successful breeders monitor the production of breeding groups by keeping records, and they replace their breeding stock with young, captive-raised animals at periodic intervals.

A female has three to four years of peak production, during which time, if she is kept under optimal conditions, she will produce six to seven clutches of eggs a year—some breeders report up to eight clutches in a peak year. That's a total of fifty-six eggs during peak production. After this, egg clutches start to decline. The example to the right (not representative in its detail, although the overall pattern is accurate) shows long-term production for a female leopard gecko. Several factors may account for production levels in a given year, but nothing changes the fact that, after seven to eight years, production drops significantly.

The maximum number of eggs a female leopard gecko can produce has not yet been determined, but is probably between ninety and one hundred. If you want to maximize production in a breeding program, retire females from the colony after seven or eight years. According to Ron Tremper, a general guideline is to retire and replace females after they have laid seventy eggs.

YEAR	EGGS
1	0
2	8
3	12
4	16
5	14
6	10
7	10
8	8
9	6
10	4
11	4
12	0
13	0

THE BUSINESS OF LEOPARD GECKOS

Making an income as a commercial herpetoculturist requires marketing and sales. If you want to produce large numbers of inexpensive geckos, lining up potential buyers, such as reptile dealers, will be important for the survival of your business. If your focus is to produce relatively small numbers of valuable morphs, then culling and selective breeding, combined with specialist target marketing, is essential. Exploring various venues for marketing, such as herpetoculture publications, reptile shows, the Internet, international markets, and direct contact, is standard homework for the successful commercial breeder.

You may think that you will sell your geckos to pet stores—which is certainly possible—but most pet stores will already have their own sources for geckos. You will need to compete with those existing sources in some way; options include selling them more cheaply, offering hatchlings at times of year when the store might have trouble getting leopard geckos elsewhere, or selling interesting morphs that are not readily available. The best way to do this is to develop a relationship with local pet stores and understand their needs before you have juvenile geckos on hand. Another option is selling online or at reptile shows.

Whatever your plan, it is unethical to breed animals unless you are fully committed to their well-being. You may have to house the young geckos yourself until you can find buyers or homes for them.

An In-Depth Look at Temperature-Dependent Sex Determination

By Brian E. Viets, PhD

In most vertebrates, sex is determined at fertilization, usually by chromosomes. This mode of sex determination is termed *genotypic sex determination* (GSD). However, in the leopard gecko and the African fat-tailed gecko, the incubation temperature of the egg determines the sex of the hatchling. This type of sex determination is termed *temperature-dependent sex determination* (TSD) and is a well-documented phenomenon occurring in all crocodilians, most turtles, and some lizards.

Both the leopard gecko and the African fat-tailed gecko have a Pattern II type of TSD; females are produced predominantly at cool temperatures, males are produced predominantly at intermediate temperatures, and females are again produced predominantly at warm temperatures. Pattern II TSD is sometimes referred to as Pattern FMF (females at cool temperatures, males at intermediate temperatures, and females at warm temperatures). For both species, some females can be produced at all temperatures; there is no set temperature that produces 100 percent males. This appears to be the norm in TSD species.

The studies that my colleagues and I perform use constant incubation temperatures, with temperatures in the incubators varying no more than 32.36°F from the desired temperature. Because these types of incubators are rarely available to hobbyists, it is important to realize the effect of varying incubation temperatures. Fluctuating incubation temperatures can substantially affect sex ratios—the greater the degree of variation, the greater the potential impact on sex ratio. In fact, the same mean incubation temperature can produce 100 percent males or 100 percent females, depending on the degree of variation from the mean.

In a species with Pattern II TSD, there are two temperatures that produce equal numbers of females and males. These two temperatures are termed *pivotal temperatures*. However, individual mothers may have very different pivotal temperatures. For instance, in leopard geckos, 87°F (31°C) typically produces an equal number of females and males.

Did You Know?

Although the leopard gecko and the African fat-tailed gecko are closely related, not all closely related geckos have the same mode of sex determination. In fact, two other closely related eublepharid geckos, the Texas banded gecko (*Coleonyx brevis*) and the banded gecko (*Coleonyx variegatus*), have GSD.

However, in some mothers, 100 percent female offspring are produced at 87°F (31°C); in others, 100 percent males are produced. (Geckos have a fixed clutch size of two eggs, so all offspring produced by a given mother in a year must be recorded. Each individual clutch can only produce two females, two males, or one of each.) The particular pattern of individual mothers may vary.

DURATION OF INCUBATION AND VIABLE INCUBATION TEMPERATURES

Incubation temperature significantly influences the duration of incubation in all lizards. In both leopard geckos and African fat-tailed geckos, incubation temperature and mean days to hatching are inversely correlated, meaning that at higher temperatures, the incubation period is shorter. In leopard geckos, the incubation period ranges from 36 days at 90.5°F (32.5°C) to 107 days at 75°F (24°C) (longer incubation periods would be expected when incubation temperature varies). At 93–95°F (34–35°C), the developmental rate slows, so the incubation period is actually longer. The lethal minimum constant incubation temperature for leopard geckos lies just below 75° F (24°C), and the lethal maximum constant incubation temperature lies just above 95°F (35°C).

HIGH INCUBATION TEMPERATURES AND FEMALE BEHAVIOR

In 1988, Gutzke and Crews reported that incubation temperature affects not only the sex but also the endocrine physiology and reproductive behavior of adult female leopard geckos. Adult females incubated at 78.8°F (26°C) (an exclusively female-producing temperature) and 84.2°F (29°C) (a mostly female-producing temperature) differed both hormonally and behaviorally from females incubated at 89.6°F (32°C) (a mostly male-producing temperature). These "hot females" were more likely to exhibit aggressive behavior, and none of them laid eggs during the study.

Two subsequent studies (Viets et al. 1993, and Tousignant et al. 1995) failed to support these findings. No hormonal differences were observed between females from different incubation temperatures, and all high-temperature females in these studies produced viable offspring.

However, incubation temperature has a profound effect on the onset of reproduction. Females from lower incubation temperatures reach sexual maturation at an earlier age than do females from higher incubation temperatures. The females in Gutzke and Crews' study were not sexually mature and therefore prematurely diagnosed as being functionally sterile.

THE EFFECTS OF INCUBATION TEMPERATURE AND HERITABILITY ON PIGMENTATION

In temperature-dependent sex determination studies on the leopard gecko, the black dorsal pigmentation varied greatly between siblings that had been incubated at 82.4°F (28°C) and 93°F (34°C). Similar variations have been reported in turtles and alligators. Thus, incubation temperature seemed to be a determining factor in the amount of black pigmentation. However, incubation temperature was not the only factor. Siblings hatched from the same temperature often had noticeable differences in the amount of black pigmentation.

In order to assess the degree to which incubation temperature affected pigmentation in leopard geckos, lizards were videotaped in a standard position, and then the images were digitized. The percentage of black pigmentation was calculated by dividing the number of black pixels by the total pixels in the image. A regression plot of the percentage of black pigmentation in hatchlings versus incubation temperature yielded a highly significant negative slope, meaning that lower incubation temperatures produced significantly darker hatchlings than did higher incubation temperatures (see graph).

However, because leopard geckos have TSD, sex and incubation temperature are confounded variables. To investigate whether sex affected pigmentation independently of incubation temperature, animals produced at 87°F (31°C)—a temperature that produces both sexes—were examined. No significant differences were found between males and females regarding the percentage of black pigmentation.

We also examined heritability of pigmentation patterns. First, we determined the amount of black pigmentation in both parents and then we compared these values with the amount of black pigmentation in their offspring. Narrow-sense heritability of black pigmentation was 27.1 percent, meaning that 27.1 percent of the pigmentation pattern of individual geckos was genetic. Darker parents tend to have darker offspring.

So, the pigmentation pattern of a gecko is due in large part to two things: the pigmentation patterns of the parents (which was expected)

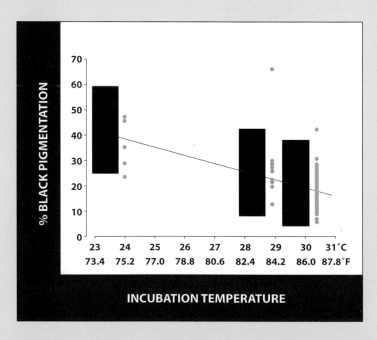

Incubation temperature is one of the factors that can play a role in black dorsal pigmentation.

and environmental effects, such as incubation temperature (which wasn't necessarily expected). Interestingly, there are other environmental factors that have an effect on pigmentation. The young, high yellow leopard gecko that you have today may turn into a mediocre-looking gecko as the breeding season wears on. Stress hormones (e.g., corticosterone) affect pigmentation, causing an animal to lose its bright coloration and become somewhat drab. Few breeding adults maintain the intensity of color that they exhibit as yearlings. In addition, studies by herpetologist Larry Talent have demonstrated that crowding (again, a stress inducer) affects pigmentation in juveniles. Hatchlings grown in crowded conditions tend to be much less colorful than those raised in isolation.

Although there are obviously some genetic components to pigmentation patterns in leopard geckos, the incubation environment, post-hatching environment, and stress of breeding can have significant effects as well. Unless you know the incubation history and lineage of a particular gecko, leopard gecko morphs should be viewed with some caution.

CHAPTER 7

THE AFRICAN FAT-TAILED GECKO

The African fat-tailed gecko is the second most widely kept and propagated eublepharid gecko. It shares many traits with its cousin, the leopard gecko. However, it has some differences, and it needs different care when kept as a pet. Fat-tailed geckos (also called fat-tails) are easy to keep and are a fine choice for a beginning keeper. A velvety appearance combined with rich, subtle coloration; large, dark eyes; and a docile personality make this species one of the best for gecko enthusiasts.

Unlike leopard geckos in the herpetoculture trade, which are only rarely taken from the wild, many fat-tailed geckos are imported into the United States out of West Africa and require careful acclimation. They usually are stressed and dehydrated from importation and carry a heavy load of parasites. A significant percentage die as a result of illness and improper care, but if carefully acclimated and properly cared for, African fat-tailed geckos are nearly as hardy as leopard geckos.

The African fat-tailed gecko (*Hemitheconyx caudicinctus*).

Captive-bred fat-tails are available, with the numbers being produced by commercial and hobbyist breeders increasing yearly. If you are new to keeping reptiles and have decided that you want a fat-tailed gecko, you are much better off starting with a captive-bred, well-started juvenile, which you will be able to find at the same places you can find leopard geckos.

WHAT'S IN A NAME?

The scientific name of the African fat-tailed gecko is *Hemitheconyx caudicinctus* (*hemi*, meaning "half" or "divided"; *theconyx*, meaning "box claw" or "nail"; and *caudicinctus*, meaning "ring-tailed"). Like the leopard gecko, the fat-tail is a eublepharid that possesses movable eyelids and lacks digital lamellae on the toes that allow other species of gecko to climb smooth surfaces, such as glass.

Fat-tailed geckos are quite prone to losing their tails. Sometimes this results from brushes with predators, but it often results from aggression by other fat-tails. This is especially true of males. When a fat-tail loses its tail, it usually grows back in a stubby, bulbous shape. The shape of the regenerated tail is the reason these lizards are called fat-tailed geckos.

FAT-TAIL DESCRIPTION

Fat-tails are more or less shaped like leopard geckos. They are a bit stockier than leopard geckos, and they grow slightly longer. Males may reach 10 inches (25 cm) in total length, and females are rarely longer than 8 inches (20 cm).

Taylor's fat-tailed gecko.

Fat-tailed geckos are banded in alternating dark and light brown. The dark bands may be rich chocolate in color, and the light bands may have a pinkish or orange tint. The dark bands are often rimmed with a thin, broken white line.

Sometimes a fat-tail will have a bright white stripe running down its back from the top of the head between the eyes to just beyond the base of the tail. This is called the *striped phase*, while the more common coloration is the *banded phase*. The striped phase is generally considered prettier by hobbyists, but both colorations make equally hardy and interesting pets. There are also several color morphs of the African fat-tailed gecko produced in captivity, including amelanistic (albino), high orange, black and white (called "oreo" in the trade), and patternless.

Like the other eublepharid geckos, fat-tailed geckos are nocturnal. They hide during the day in burrows or under objects. At night, they emerge to hunt insects and other invertebrates. When actively pursuing prey, many fat-tails twitch or wave their tails, much like leopard geckos do. They will bark and/or hiss when they feel threatened.

SEXING

Like male leopard geckos, male fat-tailed geckos are territorial. Two males in the same cage will fight, and they are very likely to injure each other. If you plan on having more than one fat-tail in a single cage, you need to know how to sex them so you avoid putting multiple males together.

The most reliable method of sexing is to turn the animal upside down and look for a V-shaped row of ten to thirteen preanal pores and the presence of hemipenal swellings at the base of the tail in males. Juvenile males can be sexed when they are a few weeks old by checking for the presence of preanal pores with a 10x magnifying glass. Males grow slightly larger than females. An adult male's head is slightly larger and broader and its neck is somewhat thicker than the female's.

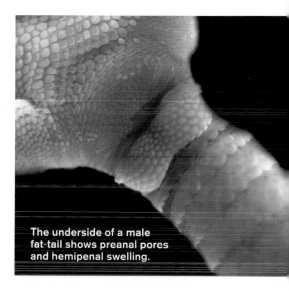

The underside of a male fat-tail shows preanal pores and hemipenal swelling.

SELECTING A FAT-TAIL

Selecting a fat-tailed gecko is much like selecting a leopard gecko—or any other reptile, for that matter. The first step to success in keeping fat-tailed geckos is to start with healthy ones. The best way to get healthy geckos is to buy captive-bred juveniles. Only experienced herpetoculturists are likely to successfully acclimate animals caught in the wild.

When selecting African fat-tailed geckos, make sure that they are active, bright-eyed, and alert, and that they have significant fat reserves in their tails. Avoid ones with thin or broken tails or with caked or smeared fecal matter around the vent area. Do not pick one that has shed skin stuck to it. It's also always a good idea to see your prospective gecko eat before you make your final decision.

ACCLIMATION

If you are a more experienced reptile keeper and want to purchase wild fat-tails to diversify your gene pool, you will have to carefully acclimate them. When acclimating a wild-caught gecko, you should be prepared to seek veterinary care. Working with a reptile veterinarian will greatly increase your chances of success.

Many imported African fat-tailed geckos are emaciated, dehydrated, stressed, and diseased. Other imported fat-tailed geckos initially look healthy but start declining in the first weeks following purchase. The following steps are required for acclimation, which can take up to two months:

1. House animals individually on paper towels in setups as described in the following section.
2. Keep the enclosures' temperature at 82–85°F (28–29°C).
3. Offer water and food as you would for a leopard gecko. Mist lightly every one to two days.
4. If a fat-tail is losing weight and becoming weak, have its stool checked by a veterinarian as soon as possible. Imported fat-tailed geckos can harbor flagellate protozoans and other causes of gastroenteritis, which will require veterinary treatment.

> ## Hydrate!
>
> With thin or debilitated animals, it is especially important to have clean water available all the time. In addition to offering water, you can rehydrate a thin fat-tail by offering one of the many electrolyte solutions now available in the reptile product trade. Try dripping the solution onto the snout with an eyedropper to incite lapping.

5. If a lizard is not readily feeding on its own, try the two following procedures.
   a. With an eyedropper, feed a mixture of banana baby food, a reptile nutritional supplement or meal powder (available at reptile specialty stores and online), and water mixed to a smooth liquid consistency. Newly imported animals usually take this mix readily, and it provides calories, water, and vitamins without the stress of force-feeding.

      To initiate ingestion of the liquid diet, apply a drop on the tip of the gecko's snout with an eyedropper. The gecko will lick the drop off and, if you bring the eyedropper close to its mouth, will start licking the liquid as you slowly push it out. Do not grab the animal and force its mouth open to pour liquid down its throat; this will do more harm than good.
   b. Another alternative, best used with animals that are relatively vigorous and have healthy body weights, is to hand-feed them one or two crickets every day. This is an easy process: kill a cricket by crushing its head with forceps and then dip it in a vitamin/mineral mix. Hold the fat-tailed gecko behind the head with one hand and poke the cricket at the side of the gecko's mouth with the other hand. When you do this, the fat-tailed gecko will probably open its mouth and try to bite sideways. When the gecko's mouth is open, insert the cricket and immediately place the gecko back in its cage. In this manner, most fat-tails will eat hand-fed crickets.

HOUSING

Housing for fat-tailed geckos is similar to that for leopard geckos. Fat-tails will thrive in the same types and sizes of cages as leopard geckos, but fat-tails require somewhat warmer and more humid conditions.

To help supply the needed humidity, use a spray bottle to mist the enclosure with water a few times each week. As with leopard geckos, females are somewhat compatible in groups, but males should never be housed together.

SUBSTRATE

Fat-tailed geckos will thrive on quite a few different substrates. Suitable substrates include newspaper, paper towels, cage carpets, recycled paper bedding, coconut husk fiber, and reptile bark substrates. All but the last two are covered in Chapter 3 of this book.

Coconut Husk Fiber

As the name implies, coconut husk fiber is made from the fibers between the inner and outer shells of coconuts. It is also called *coir*. Originally used in horticulture, it has become a popular substrate for keeping reptiles, amphibians, and arachnids.

The coir sold in pet stores for use in herp keeping is normally found in the form of compressed bricks, which need to be soaked in water before use. When soaked, the fibers absorb the water and the brick expands to many times its original size. Once soaked and broken up, it is soft and somewhat resembles peat moss.

The benefits of coconut husk fiber are that it is soft, highly absorbent, resistant to rot, and relatively

A brilliant high yellow leucistic African fat-tail.

environmentally friendly (it's compostable). Coir does not need to be changed as often as many other substrates. It also does not seem to cause impaction or other health problems for reptiles. This substrate allows fat-tails to dig burrows; to support this aspect of the substrate, mix it with a small amount (about 20 percent) of sand.

There are few disadvantages to this substrate. It has a strong, earthy odor that some keepers may find objectionable. It's not a cheap substrate, although this problem is somewhat mitigated by the fact that you will not need to replace it as often as most other options.

Reptile Bark

Various types of shredded bark are sold as reptile bedding; similar shredded barks are also sold for horticulture. Of these, the most commonly used for reptiles is orchid bark.

Bark substrates hold humidity fairly well and give gecko enclosures a natural look. You can dispose of them in compost or by using as mulch in the garden. Depending on the size of the pieces, they may pose a risk of impaction. Some varieties get moldy fast; others, such as orchid bark, do not

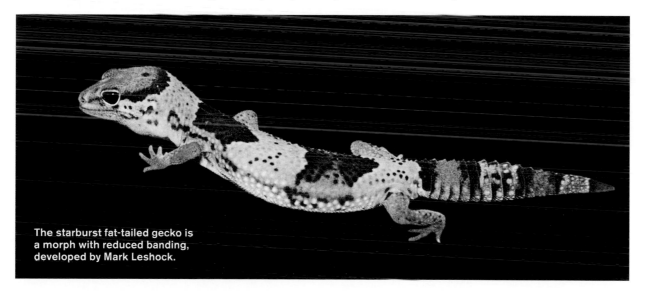

The starburst fat-tailed gecko is a morph with reduced banding, developed by Mark Leshock.

SHELTER

Fat-tailed geckos require places to hide. Any of the hide boxes recommended for leopard geckos in Chapter 3 will work for fat-tails. There should be at least one hide in the warm end of the enclosure and one in the cool end. If you are housing multiple fat-tails together, have at least one hide for each gecko plus one extra.

Because fat-tailed geckos require higher humidity than leopard geckos, at least one, if not all, of the hide boxes should be a humidified shelter. You can easily make a humidified shelter by filling a shallow container, such as the bottom of a small plastic deli container or margarine tub, with moistened sand, sphagnum moss, or coconut husk. Place the container in the tank and cover it with a much larger shelter, either plastic or clay. The inside of the shelter will then consist of an outer dry area and a central damp area. With this type of shelter, fat-tailed geckos will be able to select the level of substrate moisture, and the air humidity inside the shelter will rise. Females will typically lay eggs in humidified shelters.

FURNISHINGS

You can decorate your fat-tail's enclosure with a range of items in addition to hide boxes, depending on how you want it to look. Pieces of wood, rocks, plants (live or fake), and resin furnishings designed for use in reptile enclosures are all suitable. Make sure any décor items have no sharp edges that could injure your geckos. Rinse all store-bought decorations thoroughly to remove any dust and debris. If you gather any wood or rocks from outdoors, clean them and thoroughly disinfect them as described in Chapter 3.

HEATING

The best systems for heating fat-tailed gecko enclosures are heat tapes or reptile heating pads that can create temperature gradients of 78–90°F (26–32°C) within the cage. At night, you can drop the temperature in the enclosure to around 75°F (24°C).

HUMIDITY

The overall habitat of wild fat-tailed geckos is semiarid. However, the geckos live in relatively humid microhabitats. This means that pet fat-tails require a moderately humid enclosure. Along with providing humidified hide boxes, you should keep the air humidity in the cage within a range of 40–60 percent.

Beautiful fat-tail morphs are capturing the interest of reptile hobbyists.

Having a humidity gauge in the cage is not necessary, but it will enable you to monitor the humidity and keep it in the proper range.

You can maintain the proper humidity range by lightly misting the cage with water a few times a week and using a substrate that holds humidity. Keeping live plants in the vivarium tends to help keep the humidity elevated as well. If your fat-tail has difficulty shedding, this is almost always a sign that the humidity is too low.

FEEDING

Feeding a fat-tailed gecko is nearly identical to feeding a leopard gecko; this information can be found in Chapter 4. Fat-tails will thrive on the same regimen of live insects with occasional pinky mice (optional). The guideline for leopard gecko prey size works for fat-tails, too: the insects should be no longer than the length of the gecko's head and no wider than half the width of the head.

Gut-load all feeders prior to feeding them to your fat-tails. Dust your feeders with multivitamin and calcium supplements approximately every third feeding for adults. For hatchlings and juveniles, dust with the supplements at every feeding.

Feed adults about three times each week. Feed hatchlings and juveniles every day or every other day. Adults will eat about five to eight crickets per meal (or the equivalent size in other insects; for example, two large silkworms would likely be enough for a meal). Feed hatchlings and juveniles as many insects as they will eat at each meal. As with leopard geckos, you can keep a shallow dish of mealworms in the enclosure at

Handling

Fat-tailed geckos as a rule are not as docile as leopard geckos. They are more skittish and apt to thrash around and try to bite when handled. Handling seems to cause most fat-tails significant stress. It is probably best to regard fat-tails as pets to watch and not touch. However, some do tolerate gentle handling quite well, especially if they have been acclimated to handling as juveniles.

all times. Remove the dish when misting because mealworms tend to drown in even the smallest amount of water.

If you plan on breeding your fat-tails, offer them newborn to one-week-old mice with their rumps dipped in calcium at least once every two weeks. An increased percentage of pink mice in the diet can help improve reproductive success.

> **Important!**
> Your fat-tails need access to clean water at all times.

BREEDING

African fat-tailed geckos are generally more difficult to breed than leopard geckos. Often, females in captivity will lay several clutches of infertile eggs. Other common problems include the embryo's death before reaching full term or failure to break out of the egg.

To successfully breed fat-tailed geckos, it's crucial that you breed only healthy animals that are of a healthy weight with plump tails and good fat reserves. Prior to breeding, keep the sexes separate. This will help ensure some excitement when the geckos are paired up with unfamiliar mates.

COOLING

Breeders obtain the most consistent success when they provide a cooling period. Most breeders cool down males and females starting in October or November for two months. It likely does not matter too much when you choose to cool them, as long as you provide consistent seasons. During the cooling period, allow the ambient temperature to drop to 68–72°F (20–22°C) while keeping the heat cable or strip on the low setting. If you use a heating pad, move it so that only a small strip is underneath the enclosure and keep it at a lower setting. During the cooling period, don't offer the animals food. Provide water but do not mist.

BREEDING SEASON

After the two-month cooling period, place the animals back on a regular maintenance schedule. Offer food to females more frequently, about every other day. Once a week, feed the geckos pink mice with the rumps dipped in calcium; this may not be strictly necessary, but it seems to increase the chances of success.

Two to three weeks after the animals are back on a normal schedule, introduce a female to an enclosure containing a single male for one day, once a week, for three weeks. Remove the females after observing successful copulation. It is a good idea to have more than one male for breeding because all males are not equally fertile.

During the breeding season, which can last several months, females can produce two to seven clutches of two eggs each. If a female is introduced to a male within a day or two of egg-laying, copulation will often follow. Females must be closely monitored during breeding. Take care to provide optimal maintenance, feeding, and watering.

EGG LAYING AND INCUBATION

Offer your African fat-tailed gecko a covered container with moistened vermiculite or sand in which to lay its eggs. Cut a hole out of the side of the container, allowing the gravid female to enter the shelter. Unfortunately, a fat-tailed gecko often buries its eggs in some other area of the enclosure, sometimes right near the heat source. It is important to check the gravid female's enclosure at least twice a day during the breeding season. Fat-tailed gecko eggs can dehydrate rapidly, and many breeders lose eggs because they fail to inspect the enclosures frequently enough. Keep on top of the situation.

Incubate fat-tailed gecko eggs in the same manner and at the same temperatures as leopard gecko eggs (see Chapter 6). As with leopard geckos, incubation temperature plays a significant role in sex determination. At an incubation temperature of 90°F (32°C), the ratio of males to females will be close to even. Incubating eggs above this temperature will result in more females than males. You will also obtain more females than males in the temperature range of 82.4–86.9°F (28–31°C).

For African fat-tailed geckos, the incubation period ranges from about 39 days at 93°F (34°C) to 72 days at 82.4°F (28°C). African fat-tailed geckos cannot tolerate the lower incubation temperatures that their more temperate relative, the leopard gecko, can. This may explain why many breeders have had difficulty with this species. The viable range of incubation temperatures for African fat-tailed geckos is from 82.4°F to 97°F (28–36°C).

A baby white-striped African fat-tailed gecko.

RAISING JUVENILES

Hatchling fat-tailed geckos are typically smaller and more delicate than hatchling leopard geckos. They should be housed individually in plastic shoeboxes and kept on either paper towels or fine-grade orchid bark. Hatchling geckos will not feed until after their first shed (three to four days after hatching). During this interim period, keep them warm and provide water in a shallow dish at all times. Mist the enclosure lightly once daily to maintain adequate relative air humidity. Provide a small shelter.

After shedding, most hatchlings will feed readily on three-week-old crickets coated with a vitamin/mineral supplement. The feeding schedule should be the same as for baby leopard geckos. Take care not to introduce too many crickets or large crickets because this can traumatize the baby lizards.

Hatchling fat-tailed geckos are shy, reclusive little creatures. Some babies may not begin feeding after their first shed. Hand-feed reluctant babies, or they may start to decline.

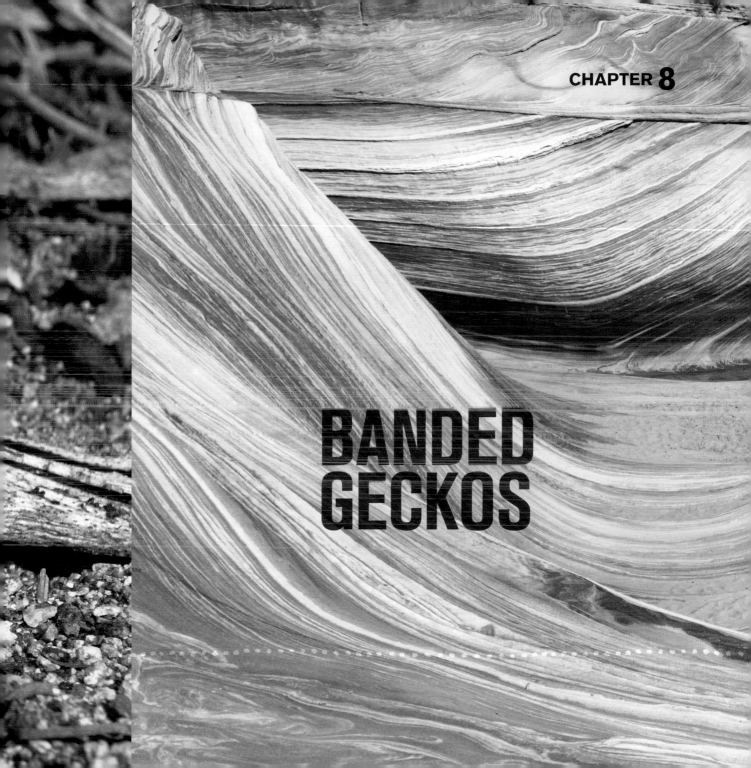

CHAPTER 8

BANDED GECKOS

Most eyelid geckos hail from parts of Asia, Africa, and Europe, but the banded geckos of the genus *Coleonyx* are an exception. This fascinating group of geckos has many similarities to leopard geckos as well as their own distinct attributes. They are not as popular or readily available as leopard geckos and fat-tailed geckos, but this doesn't mean that they don't make good pets. For the right owners, banded geckos are rewarding pets, and they are especially good for hobbyists interested in setting up naturalistic desert vivaria.

DESCRIPTION

As a whole, banded geckos look similar to leopard geckos. They are more slender and do not get as long as leopard geckos. The largest *Coleonyx* species, *C. mitratus*, reaches a maximum length of 7.5 inches (19 cm). The banded gecko's head is narrower than those of leopard and fat-tailed geckos, and the banded gecko's original tail is quite slender when compared to the tail of the leopard gecko. Like other eyelid geckos, the banded gecko regrows lost tails, and the regrown tail is usually fatter and shorter than the original.

Coleonyx mitratus, the Central American banded gecko.

The pattern of banded geckos varies across species. In general, the geckos are tan to yellow with darker bands. In several species, the bands break into numerous spots as the lizard ages.

Like leopard geckos and most other eublepharids, banded geckos are nocturnal, although the Yucatan banded gecko and the Central American banded gecko are occasionally active during the day. They spend their days in burrows or under rocks, fallen leaves, pieces of bark, or even garbage, such as old shingles or pieces of cardboard.

They prey on small insects, spiders, and other invertebrates, and they wave their tails back and forth when they are stalking prey. Given their small size, banded geckos can fall victim to a wide range of predators, including snakes, larger lizards, tarantulas, birds, toads, and possibly certain mammals, including kit foxes, coyotes, raccoons, and more.

Banded geckos are quite vocal. When they feel threatened or harassed—such as when handled or if whatever they are sheltering under is moved—they will emit a raspy noise that sounds like a combination of a hiss and a squeak. The desert banded geckos with which the junior author worked would hiss whenever he misted them.

ORIGINS AND SPECIES

Currently, seven species of *Coleonyx* are recognized, and three of these species have subspecies. The species are as follows: *C. brevis*, Texas banded gecko; *C. elegans*, Yucatan banded gecko or elegant banded gecko; *C. fasciatus*, black banded gecko; *C. mitratus*, Central American banded gecko; *C. reticulatus*, reticulate banded gecko; *C. switaki*, Switak's banded gecko; and *C. variegatus*, western banded gecko.

Not all banded gecko species are available in the pet trade. Two species, the reticulate banded gecko and Switak's banded gecko, are legally protected and therefore completely unavailable as pets. Mexico

> ### There Goes the Tail
>
> Banded geckos are very prone to losing their tails. Wild-caught banded geckos will often have regenerated tails. Tail loss can happen with even gentle handling. They also lose their tails during squabbles with tankmates. If your banded gecko loses its tail, it is usually not something to worry about. If you are providing the gecko with proper housing and excellent nutrition, it will grow a new tail soon.

does not export its wildlife, so the black banded gecko is also unavailable legally. The remaining four species are found in the pet trade and are captive bred in small numbers.

Banded geckos are found in the southwestern United States, Mexico, and Central America. They are found as far east as central Texas and occur to the west coast of California and Mexico. The northernmost limit of their range is just over the southern border of Utah. *Coleonyx* ranges as far south as Costa Rica. The species of the United States and northern Mexico—*C. brevis*, *C. fasciatus*, *C. reticulatus*, *C. switaki*, and *C. variegatus*—mostly inhabit deserts and arid mountains. The Central American species—*C. elegans* and *C. mitratus*—dwell in tropical forests.

Of the seven species of banded gecko seen in the pet trade—*C. brevis*, *C. elegans*, *C. mitratus*, and *C. variegatus*—all four are captive bred in small numbers by hobbyists, with captive-bred *C. mitratus* and *C. variegatus* usually the most frequently available. Some American hobbyists living in the western states collect their own banded geckos from the wild. The different states have different laws governing

Coleonyx variegatus bogerti, the Tucson banded gecko.

The rare reticulate banded gecko.

this practice, so you will need to verify the particulars with your state wildlife agency if you wish to collect your own geckos.

Because three species of banded gecko are currently unavailable as pets (and are likely to remain so for the foreseeable future), the following discussion of the individual species will cover only *C. brevis*, *C. elegans*, *C. mitratus*, and *C. variegatus*.

Acclimating Wild-Caught Geckos

Although captive-bred banded geckos are available, most of the banded geckos seen in the pet trade are wild-caught. These will often be suffering from stress, dehydration, and parasites. If you obtain wild-caught banded geckos, you can acclimate them much like wild fat-tailed geckos, allowing for differences in size and natural habitat. See Chapter 7 for this information.

TEXAS BANDED GECKO

The Texas banded gecko (*C. brevis*) is the smallest of the banded geckos, reaching a length of no more than 4 inches (10 cm), of which nearly half is the tail. As the common name implies, its range includes central and western Texas. It also occurs in southern New Mexico and northern Mexico in the states of Chihuahua, Coahuila, Durango, and Nuevo Leon. They live in deserts, arid grasslands, and scrub forest and are often found in canyons and gullies, sheltering in crevices and under rocks.

C. *brevis*, the Texas banded gecko.

Adult Texas banded geckos are marked in alternating bands of pale yellow and a variable pinkish brown with darker spots scattered over the entire dorsal surface. The legs are pinkish brown and usually unspotted. Like other geckos in this family, baby Texas banded geckos have solid bands with no spotting.

YUCATAN BANDED GECKO

The Yucatan banded gecko (*C. elegans*) seems to be the least available of the species found in the pet trade. Much of its natural range occurs in countries that do not export their fauna, so few of the lizards enter the trade from wild collection. A few hobbyist and professional breeders produce this species sporadically. Because *C. elegans* is a pretty and interesting gecko and because it is not readily available to hobbyists, more efforts to breed the species are warranted.

C. elegans can reach a total length of 7 inches (18 cm), making it one of the larger banded geckos. The Yucatan banded gecko might be the most attractive member of this genus. Adults have a red-brown base color with bands of bright yellow on the dorsal surface. The yellow bands have distinct black borders. There are additional dark brown to black spots on the base color.

These lizards are quite variable: in some, the bands are broken up; in others, the bands meld to form stripes. The thickness of the bands varies, too. The base color can be more orange or have a pinkish tint. All in all, Yucatan banded geckos are quite pretty, and there is enough variation to fuel interesting breeding projects with the availability of adequate stock.

This species is found as far north as the Mexican states of Nayarit and San Luis Potosi and as far south as the nation of El Salvador. The range includes much of the Yucatan Peninsula, Belize, and Guatemala. It is possible that the species occurs in Honduras as well. There are two subspecies, *C. e. elegans* and *C. e. nemoralis*. Some small differences in the scalation (arrangement of scales) of the two subspecies set them apart. Because *C. e. nemoralis* is restricted to Mexico, which does not export wildlife, it is unlikely that this subspecies is in the pet trade.

CENTRAL AMERICAN BANDED GECKO

The Central American banded gecko (*C. mitratus*) is likely the largest of the banded geckos, able to reach just over 7.5 inches (19 cm) in total length. The pattern of this species is similar to that of the other banded geckos. Its bands are more broken up, giving it a more mottled appearance. The light-colored band at the base of the skull remains distinct on most individuals.

C. mitratus occurs from Guatemala and El Salvador south to Costa Rica. It can be found in lowland forest to elevations up to 4,700 feet. The mountains of Central America split this species into two populations that may be isolated from each other; currently, the populations are not considered separate subspecies. *C. mitratus* has been found in a variety of habitats, including both wet and dry forests.

Imports may require veterinary treatment for parasites, but, once established, this is a hardy and easily maintained species.

WESTERN BANDED GECKO

Herpetologists recognize five distinct subspecies of western banded geckos: *Coleonyx variegatus abbotti*, San Diego banded gecko; *C. v. bogerti*, Tucson banded gecko; *C. v. sonoriensis*, Sonoran banded gecko; *C. v. utahensis*, Utah banded gecko; and *C. v. variegatus*, desert banded gecko. Several other subspecies

C. v. variegatus, the western banded gecko.

were formerly recognized, so you may run into other names when researching this species. The subspecies differ slightly in their patterns and their native ranges. In many areas, there are geckos that show evidence of interbreeding between the subspecies; these are called *intergrades*. The two subspecies that seem to be most common in the pet trade are the Tucson and the desert banded geckos. As a whole, this species is found from west-central California and southern Utah south into Mexico, including Sonora and the Baja Peninsula.

Western banded geckos reach a maximum total length of around 6 inches (15 cm). Because they have the scientific name *Coleonyx variegatus*, you might expect them to be variable in appearance—and you would be correct. In most cases, the geckos have bands of pale to bright yellow on a background of pink to light brown. The thickness of the bands varies greatly. Many have darker spots on the body. In some, the bands break up as the animals age, leaving them more speckled or mottled than banded.

This species is found in many different arid and semiarid habitats within their range. They are most often found in association with rocks but are also seen in sandy dunes and open forests. Western banded geckos often hold their tails up in an arch over their backs when they move about. It is believed that they are mimicking the appearance of scorpions. This species is known to eat scorpions, along with the more typical insects, millipedes, and small invertebrates.

All in the Genus

There are seven species of *Coleonyx* recognized by herpetologists. Three of these species have subspecies. Here is a complete list of the species and subspecies.

Coleonyx brevis, Texas banded gecko

Coleonyx elegans, Yucatan banded gecko or elegant banded gecko

> *Coleonyx elegans elegans*

> *Coleonyx elegans nemoralis*

Coleonyx fasciatus, black banded gecko

Coleonyx mitratus, Central American banded gecko

Coleonyx reticulatus, reticulate banded gecko

Coleonyx switaki, Switak's banded gecko

> *Coleonyx switaki gypsicolus*

> *Coleonyx switaki switaki*

Coleonyx variegatus, western banded gecko

> *Coleonyx variegatus abbotti*, San Diego banded gecko

> *Coleonyx variegatus bogerti*, Tuscon banded gecko

> *Coleonyx variegatus sonoriensis*, Sonoran banded gecko

> *Coleonyx variegatus utahensis*, Utah banded gecko

> *Coleonyx variegatus variegatus*, desert banded gecko

HOUSING

In terms of care, banded geckos can be divided roughly into two groups: the North American species and the Central American species. The first group includes the Texas banded and western banded geckos (plus the black banded, reticulate banded, and Switak's banded geckos, should they ever become available to hobbyists). The Central American species are the Yucatan banded and Central American banded geckos. The North American species are desert dwellers, while the Central American species come from more humid environments.

All species of banded gecko will fare well in housing approximately the size of a 5- or 10-gallon (19- or 38-liter)aquarium. In a 10-gallon (38-liter) enclosure, you can keep a trio of banded geckos as long as only one male is in the group.

A Texas banded gecko checks rock crevices for prey.

SUBSTRATE

The desert-dwelling North American species can be kept much like leopard geckos, so a substrate of newspaper, paper towels, cage carpet, recycled paper bedding, or sand works for them. Sand is the most common choice for these geckos because it mimics their natural environment.

The Central American species can be kept more like fat-tailed geckos. The substrate choices for them include newspaper, paper towels, cage carpet, recycled paper bedding, coconut husk, and reptile bark; the substrates that hold humidity are best for these species. A blend of coconut husk and sand works well for them. If you use a substrate that does not hold humidity well, you will need to mist these geckos to maintain humidity.

Banded geckos of all species will dig shallow burrows. To encourage this, keep them on a substrate that enables them to dig, such as sand, coconut husk, or recycled paper bedding, at a depth of at least 3 inches (8 cm). Place any rocks, branches, or other cage furnishings on the bottom of the cage, not on top of the substrate, so that the geckos cannot tunnel under the items with the risk of the items collapsing onto the geckos.

Given the small size of the banded geckos, they make excellent inhabitants of naturalistic vivaria. The North American species can be kept in desert vivaria like those described for leopard geckos in Chapter 3. The Central American species will need vivaria with higher humidity levels, which means that any plants housed with these geckos must be able to tolerate the same conditions

HEATING AND HUMIDITY

Despite being from hot regions, banded geckos spend their days in cooler microhabitats and are active mainly at night, when temperatures drop. Because of their preference for relatively cooler temperatures, you don't need to keep banded geckos very hot. Keep the hottest spot of the enclosure between 82–85°F (28–29°C) and the coolest spot around 75°F (24°C). At night, you can drop the temperatures to 72 to 75°F (22–24°C). Any of the heating methods discussed in Chapter 3 will successfully maintain the proper temperatures for banded geckos.

Caution!

Although some hobbyists use sphagnum moss to maintain humidity, others have had banded geckos suffer impactions from this substrate, so it is not recommended.

For the North American species, keep the cage dry overall but provide them with humidified shelters (see the next section, "Hiding Places"). The Central American species need higher humidity. Along with providing humidified shelters, mist the cage daily, preferably in the evening. Maintain air humidity for these two species at 70–80 percent.

HIDING PLACES

Banded geckos hide for most of the day and will do well with any of the shelter types recommended for leopard geckos in Chapter 3, taking into account the smaller size of the banded geckos. Like the other eublepharid geckos, *Coleonyx* do best when given at least one humidified shelter. This can be a small, covered plastic food container with some moistened coconut husk or sand in it and a hole cut in the side for the geckos to enter and exit.

> **Did You Know?**
>
> Having at least one shelter per gecko is ideal, but banded geckos will often crowd into the same hide box.

You can also moisten the substrate beneath half of a log, a piece of cork bark, or a similar shelter either by misting the area beneath the shelter daily or by pouring a little water into the substrate as needed. If you lift the substrate and mist beneath it, be prepared for the gecko to object vocally with a squeaky hiss.

> **Hands Off**
>
> The banded geckos are small, slight, and delicate. It is easy to injure one when handling it. Additionally, most of them do not adapt well to handling and suffer great stress when handled. It is best to think of them as pets to watch rather than handle.

FEEDING AND WATERING

Like all of the other eublepharid geckos, banded geckos are insectivores. They will eat any small, live invertebrates that they can catch. In captivity, they can be fed much like leopard geckos, but their food must be smaller than that for leopard geckos. Two-week-old crickets and other insects of approximately the same size are generally fine for adult banded geckos. Gut-load and supplement all prey items as discussed in Chapter 4.

Banded geckos are aggressive feeders, stalking and attacking their prey with gusto. They seem to require more food for their size than do leopard and fat-tailed geckos. Keep an eye on their appearance to be sure you are feeding them enough food—but not too much.

Banded geckos should have access to clean water at all times. Due to their size, take care with the water bowl you select. A jar lid may be the best option. The geckos will also lick up water from misting.

BREEDING

Banded geckos are not captive bred in any sizable numbers. Breeding these little gems is a worthwhile endeavor for hobbyists who have a little experience breeding leopards or fat-tails, keeping in mind that *Coleonyx* species are somewhat more challenging to breed than leopards and fat-tails. This is in part due to their smaller size and in part due to their being not as well understood as the other two species. A fairly high percentage of clutches fail to hatch, and the reasons for this are not known.

C. v. bogerti, the Tucson banded gecko.

SEXING

Adult banded geckos are rather easy to sex. A male has a pair of spur-like projections on the underside of the base of the tail, just past the vent. Additionally, the area posterior to the vent is enlarged and looks swollen.

COOLING PERIOD

Breeders of the North American banded geckos have the most consistent success when they subject their geckos to a seasonal cooling period of about two months. Most breeders cool their geckos during the North American winter months to match the natural rhythms that the geckos would follow in the wild. The Central American species do not seem to require these seasonal variations to breed.

The required temperature range during cooling is 63–70°F (17–21°C). Drop the temperature gradually over two to four weeks. During this time, do not feed the geckos in order to prevent food from going undigested during the simulated winter, which can cause serious illness. The lizards still need access to water at this time. They will likely be sluggish and rarely come out of hiding while they are being cooled.

After the desired cooling period, turn the heat back on and raise the temperatures up to normal over the span of a few days. The geckos will begin feeding again shortly. Feed them very well—especially the females—throughout the breeding season.

MATING AND GESTATION

Within a few weeks of returning to normal temperatures, the geckos should begin mating. You may not see them in action because most of the activity will occur at night. Once mating is successful, females will start laying in a few weeks. Banded geckos are very prolific in captivity, laying up to eleven clutches a year.

EGG LAYING AND INCUBATION

Banded geckos will use nesting boxes similar to the ones described for leopard geckos in Chapter 6. Use an appropriately sized box; a female may reject a box that is too roomy. As with other geckos, check the enclosure frequently for eggs laid outside the box. Banded gecko eggs are tiny, so look carefully and be very careful when moving them from the nesting box to the incubation container.

Eggs can be incubated like leopard gecko eggs at 78–82°F (26–28°C). Unlike leopard geckos and fat-tailed geckos, banded geckos do not have temperature-dependent sex determination, so the sex of the hatchlings is unaffected by the incubation temperatures. Incubation time varies with temperature and species but averages about eight weeks.

HATCHLING CARE

The young of all banded gecko species are very attractive in velvety brown with high-contrast, pale-yellow bands. They are also quite tiny, and the hatchlings' small size poses several challenges to the breeder. The first and most obvious is providing them with food that is small enough for them to eat. Many pet stores will not carry insects that hatchling banded geckos can eat. Online suppliers are the best bet. It is wise to lay in a supply before the hatchlings arrive. Some options include pinhead crickets, flightless fruit flies, bean beetles, flour beetle larvae, mini-mealworms, and hatchling silkworms. Make sure that the hatchlings consume all of the food at each feeding. Hatchling banded geckos are especially prone to being attacked by uneaten crickets.

The tiny hatchlings also dehydrate quickly. Mist them a few times daily. If you put a water bowl in the enclosure, keep it small and shallow to ensure that these small lizards cannot drown in it.

Another challenge is handling the babies because their small size makes them delicate, and they are quite prone to injury when being handled. A good method is to gently herd them into a cup instead of trying to pick them up by hand.

Did You Know?

Selectively breeding banded geckos, as with leopard geckos, could result in beautiful morphs. Currently, no banded-gecko morphs are known.

CHAPTER 9

OTHER EYELID GECKOS

Besides the leopard, fat-tailed, and banded geckos, there are several other lizards in the eyelid gecko family, including African clawed geckos (*Holodactylus*), cat geckos (*Aeluroscalabotes*), and cave geckos (*Goniurosaurus*). None of these species are common in the pet trade; in fact, except for some of the cave geckos, they are quite rare. All of these species are best left to experienced hobbyists.

The African clawed gecko (*Holodactylus africanus*).

The species covered in this chapter are rarely available as captive-bred individuals. Individuals seen in the pet trade are often dehydrated, stressed, and carrying parasites. They will need expert husbandry and often veterinary care in order to successfully adapt to life in captivity. Mortality of these imported lizards can be high.

One of the issues with these lizards is that their habitat and natural behaviors are poorly studied. It's difficult to provide proper captive conditions when their basic needs are not fully known. Current information is provided here, but readers should expect that new research and more captive experience will change our understanding of what these animals need in captivity.

AFRICAN CLAWED GECKO

Every so often, small numbers of the African clawed gecko (*Holodactylus africanus*) are imported from East Africa, most often from Tanzania. In the wild, they are commonly found in sandy washes and gullies. This is a small eublepharid with very large eyes that digs burrows. Imported *H. africanus* need expert care—often including treatment for parasites—if they are to adapt to captivity. Quite often, they seem to adapt to life as a pet but then stop eating and die after less than a year. These odd and reclusive little creatures are best left to specialists.

DESCRIPTION

African clawed geckos reach a maximum size of 4 inches (10 cm) total length, and most will be just over 3 inches (around 8 cm). Males get slightly larger than females. In body shape, clawed geckos look much like leopard geckos with short, spearhead-shaped tails. They have proportionally shorter legs and larger heads than leopard geckos. Their eyes are particularly large, with pale yellow eyelids that accentuate the eyes.

The color of these lizards is less than stunning, but their pattern is subtle and interesting. They are overall a rich brown broken by bands of brownish purple. The bands are irregularly shaped and often have paler centers. The light brown areas of the pattern have irregular pale spots and squiggles. In most of those seen in the hobby, a faint white stripe runs down the spine, usually to the tail tip, and overlays the rest of the pattern. The stripe forks to a Y shape at the nape and ends just behind the eyes.

What's in a Name?

Holodactylus africanus is normally referred to as the African clawed gecko (or, occasionally, the African fingered gecko) by hobbyists. These names are vague and not terribly descriptive. Almost all geckos have claws, and no geckos really have fingers. The junior author of this book has suggested using the name *gully geckos* because they are most often found in dry streambeds, gullies, washes, and similar habitats.

The African clawed gecko is best left to experts.

There are four toes on each foot. For unknown reasons, the outer toes and bottoms of the feet are gray and the inner toes are white. Like other eyelid geckos, *Holodactylus* lacks toe pads and the ability to climb smooth surfaces.

Clawed geckos are strongly nocturnal. They rarely leave their burrows before nightfall. In captivity, they will come out of their burrows every third or fourth night to hunt for food. They will occasionally stick their heads up above the sand, which can give the impression that there is just a gecko head sitting on the ground.

The Other *Holodactylus*

There is one other species of *Holodactylus*, *H. cornii*. This species is rarely seen in nature and is poorly known to biologists. There is almost no information available on this species. It is similar in size, coloration, and habitat to *H. africanus*. It is found in Somalia with a range that is believed to be completely separated from that of *H. africanus*. It does not appear that this species has ever been found in the reptile hobby.

A savannah in Serengeti National Park in Tanzania, the country from which African clawed geckos are most frequently imported.

RANGE AND HABITAT

African clawed geckos are found in East Africa along the borders of Kenya and Tanzania into Ethiopia; they possibly also occur in Somalia. Their distribution is discontinuous across this area. The geckos seem to be primarily found in gullies, washes, and dry streambeds. Their habitat is arid savannahs and deserts in a region with a short rainy season in the late spring to early summer.

These lizards dig deep burrows and do not stray far from them. They will often dig their burrows at the base of termite mounds, although it is not known if they eat the termites. Captives will certainly feast on these insects.

CARE

Clawed geckos are not available as captive-bred animals. You will need to select yours carefully to avoid geckos that are already too stressed and sickened by capture and importation to adapt to captivity. Much of the selection guidelines that work for leopard geckos will work here as well: look for geckos that have good weight, are alert, have no obvious wounds, and have no fecal material caked on the vent. If possible, watch them eat and select those that show good appetites and normal hunting behaviors.

Because these lizards so often carry internal parasites, taking them to a veterinarian soon after purchase is recommended. Bring a fresh stool sample from each gecko with you. You may also want to set them up in simplified housing so you can better observe them (and their droppings) for a few weeks until they acclimate. (See Chapter 3 for quarantine and simplified housing information.)

Housing

Clawed geckos are small and do not roam too much; thus, they can be kept in fairly small setups. A trio will be completely happy in an enclosure the size of a 10-gallon (38 liter) tank (20 x 11 x 13 inches [51 x 28 x 33 cm]). As with other eyelid geckos, never house more than one male in a given enclosure.

Burrowing is central to the natural behavior of clawed geckos. A substrate that allows them to dig their extensive burrows is best for them. Use sand or a mix of sand and coconut husk at a depth of at least 3 inches (8 cm).

Although clawed geckos are found in dry habitats, their burrows stay relatively humid. They will do best when provided a similar environment in captivity, which you can achieve by pouring water in one corner of the enclosure to create a locally moist area in an otherwise dry habitat. Another option is to prop up a piece of PVC piping or other type of tube vertically so that it extends beneath the substrate. Pour water down this pipe so that only the bottom layers of sand are moistened. Lastly, you can keep some live desert plants in the cage with their pots buried in the substrate. When you water the plants, the drainage will moisten the bottom of the substrate. No matter which method you choose, keep at least half the enclosure dry.

Include a few pieces of cork bark, cholla cactus skeleton, or other hiding places for the geckos. They will likely tunnel under them, so be sure that they cannot crush your geckos. You can also use rocks for decoration.

Cleaning these geckos' enclosures is fairly easy because they generally choose a corner as a toilet and deposit their droppings only in that spot. Scoop the soiled substrate out of that corner on a weekly basis and replace all of the substrate about every six months.

Heating

Clawed geckos will spend almost all of their time underground. In nature, their burrows would be much cooler than the surface, so they burrow to escape heat and reach the temperature they prefer. This behavior makes the use of under-tank heating potentially dangerous. The geckos may burrow to escape the heat, but if the heat is coming from their burrows, they may become too hot. Having to choose between staying in the burrow and overheating or being out in the open and at the right temperature will cause the lizards stress and adversely impact their health.

It is therefore best to heat these geckos with an overhead heat lamp. The spot directly under the heat lamp should be 85–90°F (29–32°C). Keep the light on the dry side of the vivarium to provide a temperature gradient. At night, the temperatures in the enclosure can drop to the low 70s (around 22–23°C).

Feeding

Clawed geckos can be fed much like other eyelid geckos. They will eat a variety of appropriately sized insects. These geckos can take larger prey for their size than other eublepharids; however, it is still best to feed them prey of the recommended size—no more than the length and less than half the width of the lizard's head—just to ensure there is no problem.

In the experience of the junior author, clawed geckos seem to eat waxworms and darkling beetles (the adult form of mealworms) most enthusiastically, but they completely ignore pill bugs. Other keepers report that their clawed geckos eat small roaches and termites well and put on weight quickly from these foods. A clawed gecko will eat more for its size at one meal than will a leopard gecko.

Waxworms are among the clawed gecko's favorite foods.

Gut-load all insects with the appropriate nutritious diet for that particular feeder species. The proper regimen for supplementation has not been determined for clawed geckos. For the time being, the best thing to do is supplement the same way as you would with leopard geckos (see Chapter 4).

Offer clawed geckos food on nights when they are moving around above the sand. If they don't come out on a given night, they are likely not hungry, and you can skip feeding them. The junior author's clawed geckos would emerge every two to three nights to hunt. Always feed this species at night when they are active.

Clawed geckos drink water only on occasion. Still, it is best to make sure they have access to fresh water at all times. They will also soak themselves in the bowl sometimes. Use a shallow bowl that the lizards can get in and out of and that is not deep enough to pose a drowning risk.

BREEDING

Despite the rarity of the species, *H. africanus* has been bred by advanced hobbyists on several occasions. One of the obstacles to breeding clawed geckos is finding females. Many more males have been imported than females. This likely means that, in nature, the males wander away from their burrows more often, probably in search of females. If that is the case, then males would be collected and exported more often than females because they are easier to find and capture.

Sexing these geckos can also be challenging. Adult males have hemipenal bulges, but the differences in the area just past the vent in males and females can be subtle. Males also have tiny spurs next to the vent, much like banded geckos do. Again, the differences can be hard to spot.

Checking the pores on the undersides of the thighs, the femoral pores, may be the best way to sex this species. You will need a magnifying glass to get a detailed look. The males will have numerous large pores, while the females will have a few small pores.

Lastly, females tend to be smaller and more slender with proportionately smaller heads than males. To make sure you are sexing the geckos accurately, the best method is to look at all of the characteristics mentioned here.

Seasonal cooling is the most reliable way to trigger breeding. Breeders have had success breeding clawed geckos by cooling the cage down to the high 70s (25–26°C) for two to three months. After returning to normal temperatures, the geckos will start mating. They seem to prefer to mate outside of the burrows but in other hiding areas. If you are housing your group all together, you may notice a female digging a new burrow away from the others. Gravid females seem to prefer to live in their own burrows.

Females may lay a few clutches of eggs per season. Clutches may have one or two eggs, often alternating between one and two as the season goes on.

Incubate the eggs with a temperature range of 82-85°F (28–29°C). It is not known if clawed geckos have temperature-dependent sex determination (TSD) or not. *Holodactylus* is most closely related to the fat-tailed geckos (*Hemitheconyx*), which does exhibit TSD. This makes it more likely than not that clawed geckos do exhibit TSD. If that is the case, and if their form of TSD is the same as that in fat-tails, the suggested temperatures will produce more females than males.

Using perlite as an incubation medium has met with more success than using sand or vermiculite. You can purchase perlite in the plant section of a nursery, garden store, or home-improvement store. To obtain the proper moisture in the perlite, soak it in water and then drain it in a colander. If it dries during the course of incubation, pour a little bit of water into the incubation container. Eggs hatch in six to eight weeks.

The hatchlings will be about .5 inch (1 cm) long. They will start eating about two days after hatching, once they have had their first shed. Before you have hatchlings, make sure you have a source of tiny insects for food. They will eat pinhead crickets, bean beetles, flour beetle (*Tribolium confusum*) larvae, hatchling silkworms, and flightless fruit flies.

CAT GECKO

The cat gecko (*Aeluroscalabotes felinus*) is undoubtedly the oddest of the eyelid geckos. It has several attributes not shared with the other members of the family Eublepharidae. It is so distinct from the others that it has been given its own subfamily, Aeluroscalabotinae. Cat geckos are avid climbers that live in the rainforests of Southeast Asia. The species is sometimes called the Malaysian cat gecko, although it is found in several other countries. While this lizard is still rare in captivity, it has become more available, and there has been more success in keeping and breeding this species.

DESCRIPTION

Female cat geckos reach a maximum total length of 7.5 inches (19 cm), with the tail accounting for about half of the length. Males are smaller; they generally get no longer than 5 inches (13 cm). The species is named *felinus* due to a few catlike attributes; one of the most interesting is that they have retractable claws. Additionally, when observing one of these lizards, you cannot help but be struck by their feline postures, movements, and grace. Cat geckos even curl their tails around them, as cats do. They are like little cold-blooded cats.

The rare cat gecko (*Aeluroscalabotes felinus*) is slowly increasing in availability.

Location, Location, Location

Cat geckos exhibit different coloration across their range, with certain colorations and other characteristics consistently seen in individual geckos coming from specific localities, creating speculation that *Aeluroscalabotes* is actually composed of several subspecies or even full species. Keepers and breeders take careful note of where their animals come from and use colloquial names for their localities and notable characteristics, such as Red Cameron Highlands, Johor Silver Eye, and Borneo Green Eye. The latter is often called *Aeluroscalabotes cf. felinus dorsalis* by keepers, the "cf." meaning that this animal may be different enough from the given species to be considered a different species. Because of the probability that unrecognized subspecies or species exist, the best practice is to breed only those cat geckos from the same locality together.

Unlike cats and unlike all other eublepharids, cat geckos have prehensile tails. Their tails can help them grip branches, which is a superb adaptation to their arboreal lifestyle. Although they are avid climbers, they lack the toe pads seen in typical geckos, so they cannot climb smooth surfaces.

Cat geckos are strongly nocturnal. In captivity, they will sleep under leaf litter on the floor of the enclosure and move up into the branches at night to hunt. It is reasonable to think that they do the same in nature, but this is not known for sure.

Currently, two subspecies of *A. felinus* are recognized: *A. felinus felinus* and *A. felinus multituberculatus*; the latter is found only on Sanana Island in Indonesia. Additionally, a cat gecko with green eyes that is likely from Borneo has been imported to Europe and the United States. Breeders have been using the names *Aeluroscalabotes cf. felinus dorsalis* and *Aeluroscalabotes aff. dorsalis* for the green-eyed animals. Many breeders believe the green-eyed cat gecko is a separate subspecies or species. Herpetologists have not reviewed the status of the different populations of cat gecko recently, so one cannot be sure how many species or subspecies of cat gecko there actually are. One of the problems with breeding the cat gecko may be that there are different species that are not reproductively compatible.

Aeluroscalabotes felinus.

RANGE AND HABITAT

Cat geckos are found in a spotty natural range that includes parts of Thailand, Cambodia, Malaysia, Singapore, and a number of Indonesian islands, including Borneo and the Sula Islands. The species is protected from export by Thailand.

Cat geckos inhabit montane forests. They live in both primary and secondary rainforests. These woodlands are cool and humid, with frequent mists and rains. Some populations are found in warmer lowland forests, but these cat geckos are always found close to running water. This species has also been found close to cultivated fields.

CARE

The care of cat geckos is quite different from the care of other species of eyelid gecko. Cat geckos require high humidity and branches or other structures they can climb.

As with the other geckos in this chapter, most of the cat geckos available are wild-caught and may not be in the best condition. If you purchase wild-caught cat geckos, quarantine and a simplified setup are recommended for the first few weeks (see Chapter 3). However, waiting to purchase cat geckos until you can find captive-bred ones is highly recommended.

Housing

With other eyelid geckos, the height of the vivarium is not an important consideration. Not so for cat geckos. This species needs the opportunity to climb. They do not need to be housed in the vertically oriented enclosures used for chameleons, but the enclosure should have enough height to allow for climbing branches. A 10-gallon (38-liter) aquarium or equivalent (20 x 11 x 13 inches [51 x 28 x 33 cm]) provides enough space for a cat gecko, and most experienced keepers recommend housing cat geckos singly outside of breeding attempts. A glass or acrylic enclosure will help maintain the high humidity that cat geckos need.

The keepers who have the most success with cat geckos are those who strive to re-create small South Asian rainforests. Keeping this species in naturalistic vivaria is highly recommended.

Substrate choices include sphagnum moss, coconut husk, orchid bark, and soil, or a mix of these. If you are using soil, you must be sure it is safe for reptiles. Most potting soils are not safe because they contain fertilizers and perlite. Organic potting soils are often safe. Serious vivarium keepers often make

Cat geckos fare best in a vivarium that recreates rainforest conditions.

ABG Soil

One of the most highly regarded soils for humid naturalistic vivaria is ABG soil. ABG stands for Atlanta Botanical Gardens, where this soil was developed. Some retailers sell ABG soil, but hobbyists can make their own with the following typical recipe.

1 part milled peat
1 part milled sphagnum moss
1 part fine charcoal
2 parts fine tree fern fiber
2 parts fine orchid bark

their own soil. There are now several good vivarium soils available commercially. Your pet store may be able order one for you, or you can get it online.

Unlike most of the other eyelid geckos, cat geckos do not burrow. This means the substrate does not need to be particularly deep. Two to three inches will suffice.

Having a drainage layer under the substrate is a good idea. The usual drainage layer used for vivaria is expanded clay aggregate (e.g., Hydroton), but a product called Growstone claims to be more environmentally friendly. You can use gravel, but it is very heavy. Fine mesh screening over the drainage layer helps keep the soil from sinking down into it.

Top off the substrate with a layer of leaf litter. You can buy leaf litter from terrarium suppliers or collect your own from pesticide-free areas. Be sure to collect only leaves that are known to be safe for reptiles. A few common trees with leaves that are safe to use in a gecko terrarium are almond, mulberry, maple, beech, chestnut, hazel, linden, and oak. Magnolia leaves are especially good; they last a long time and curl up a bit, creating hiding places for the geckos. You will also need to sort through the leaves to pick out anything undesirable: animal droppings, galls, thorns, pests, and such. You can rinse the leaves, too, if you like.

You can place live plants directly in the vivarium soil. Choose plants that will thrive in humid conditions and that are sturdy enough to withstand geckos climbing on them. A few suggestions are pothos, philodendrons, some types of ficus, and some types of ferns. If you are using live plants, provide them with adequate light.

Along with the plants, furnish your cat gecko enclosure with some climbing branches and hiding places. Cork bark rounds and flats make excellent hides.

Heat and Humidity

Cat geckos do not need an overly warm environment. They do well with a daytime temperature range of 75–82°F (24–28°C). If kept above 84°F (29°C) for any length of time, cat geckos often die. At night, temperatures can drop to as low as 65°F (18°C) safely. Often, the UVB lighting will generate enough heat to keep the enclosure within this temperature range without a supplemental heating source.

High humidity is critical for the health of cat geckos. They require relative humidity of 80–90 percent almost constantly. You should purchase a hygrometer to measure the humidity within the enclosure.

To maintain humidity as high as cat geckos need it, you will need to spray the enclosure nightly. You may want to invest in a misting system or humidifier. If using a hand mister, try to

> **Important!**
>
> Always wash plants off before including them in an enclosure. Unless you buy them from a company that supplies plants specifically for use with herps, rinse all the soil off the roots to ensure that you aren't introducing any harmful fertilizers or pesticides to the vivarium.

> **Did You Know?**
>
> Most successful keepers provide UVB lighting for their cat geckos. See chapter 3 for a discussion of UVB and geckos.

avoid spraying the geckos directly because it seems to cause them stress. Some keepers partially cover the screen top of their geckos' enclosures with plastic or glass to help hold humidity in. Live plants and a soil substrate will help maintain proper humidity.

Feeding

Cat geckos will feed on a variety of appropriately sized insects. Prey items should be about 90 percent of the size of the gecko's head.

You can feed any of the prey items discussed in Chapter 4 to cat geckos, but cat geckos have a reputation for being fussy about their food. Many keepers report that their cat geckos seem to really enjoy isopods (wood lice), which you can harvest from outdoors or purchase from specialty reptile-supply vendors. Some keepers recommend feeding breeding females small snails because the shells provide extra calcium.

A rainforest in Thailand, where the cat gecko is protected from import.

Feed cat geckos in small amounts. Do not feed more than two or three insects in a feeding. Offer food roughly every other night and remove any uneaten food each morning. Insects wandering about the enclosure can cause cat geckos stress.

Some keepers report that cat geckos are sensitive to oversupplementation. To reduce the risk, it may be best to dust prey with supplements only once or twice a month. All feeder insects should be appropriately gut-loaded.

BREEDING

Successful captive breeding of cat geckos is still a rarity. There is much to learn about their biology, needs, and reproduction.

Male cat geckos have hemipenal bulges that are usually easy to see. Additionally, you can be reasonably certain that any cat gecko that is more than 6 inches (15 cm) long is a female.

Some breeders recommend a cooling period for cat geckos, while others keep them at the same temperature year round. If you use a cooling period, it should last for about two months. During the cooling period, daytime temperatures should get no warmer than 72°F (22°C), and nighttime temperatures can be as low as 60°F (16°C).

After the cooling period, move the male into the female's enclosure. The male can stay there for two to four weeks, but if you see that the female is gravid or if it seems as if either gecko is causing stress to the other, move the male back to his own cage. Herpetologists have reported that females can store and use sperm for a year or longer after a successful mating.

Like most other geckos, female cat geckos usually lay two eggs in a clutch, and they lay four to six clutches per year. They prefer to lay their eggs on the ground under bark or leaves. When you see that the female is gravid, check the cage for eggs daily. You may want to reduce the number of likely egg-laying spots to just a few that you can easily monitor. Once you find eggs, move them to an incubation chamber without turning them.

Most breeders use perlite or vermiculite for their incubation medium, which must be moist but not overly wet. Use distilled or reverse-osmosis water for incubation. Herpetologists have not yet definitely determined the best temperatures for incubating cat geckos' eggs, but keeping the eggs at the same temperatures as for other geckos generally works. Temperatures on the lower end of the normal range for keeping tends to produce larger and heartier hatchlings. The eggs can take 60 to 120 days to hatch, with lower temperatures resulting in longer incubation times.

Hatchlings are about 3 inches (8 cm) long. They can be kept in the same type of setup as adults, although a substrate of paper towels may be better than soil for the first few months to avoid impactions. Keep hatchlings together in a 10-gallon (38-liter) enclosure for several months. Feed insects that are about 90 percent of the geckos' head size. Offer food nightly, removing uneaten prey in the morning. Because these geckos are sensitive to mineral supplementation, it may be best to dust the hatchlings' prey with supplements at only every third or fourth feeding. The best supplementation schedule for cat geckos is one of the mysteries of their care still waiting to be solved.

CAVE GECKOS

The cave geckos are a complicated group of species that comprise the genus *Goniurosaurus*. These lizards are found under many names, including Asian, Chinese, Japanese, and Vietnamese leopard geckos and Chinese, Japanese, and Vietnamese cave geckos. Many hobbyists call them *gonis*, a name derived by shortening the genus name. Whatever they are called, these geckos are interesting, attractive, and highly sought after.

Herpetologists recognize seventeen species of *Goniurosaurus*, many of which were once considered subspecies but have been elevated to full species status following more thorough research. Their habitat preference has contributed to complicated speciation. They inhabit caves, rocky outcroppings, and limestone crevices in wet forests. With such specific habitat requirements, it is common for small populations to become isolated

The cave gecko
Goniurosaurus hainensis.

from others. After enough time with little genetic input from other populations, the isolated groups become their own species.

This tangle of species is usually divided into three major groups, with a few species left over. The groups are named after three species that typify each group: the Luii, Lichtenfelderi, and Kuroiwae groups. Four species that have been more recently researched are not assigned to any of these groups and are not known to be in the reptile trade.

Gonis first became popular in the 1990s, with a great surge of interest by keepers and breeders in the early 2000s. Unfortunately, increased interest has led to overcollection of several species, and several local and national governments now protect various species. For these reasons, along with the better chance of success at keeping and breeding them, prospective keepers are advised to seek out captive-bred gonis, which continue to become more available with each passing year.

DESCRIPTION

Gonis look much like leopard geckos at first glance but they are actually more slender, with a spindly appearance. Cave geckos have narrower heads than most of the other eyelid geckos. They have well-developed claws, but, like other eublepharids, they lack toe pads.

Cave geckos vary in color between species and population, but most are banded in contrasting colors that can include brown, purple, pink, and yellow. The bands may be well defined, faint, or broken into irregular blotches and spots. Most species have ringed original tails, but regenerated tails are often blotchy. Size varies by species and species group. Cave geckos are noted for their richly colored eyes, ranging through amber, gold, orange, and red.

The Luii Group

Six species make up the Luii group: *Goniurosaurus araneus, G. bawanglingensis, G. catbaensis, G. huuliensis, G. luii,* and *G. yingdeensis.* Several of these were once considered subspecies of *G.luii.* They are all found in humid montane forests.

G. araneus is known as the Vietnamese leopard gecko, Vietnamese cave gecko, and Vietnamese tiger gecko in the reptile hobby. The species is found in northern Vietnam and adjacent areas of China. The

Cave Gecko Species

There are seventeen species of cave gecko in the genus *Goniurosaurus*. A complete list of the species and their group assignments follow.

Luii group:

Goniurosaurus araneus

Goniurosaurus bawanglingensis

Goniurosaurus catbaensis

Goniurosaurus huuliensis

Goniurosaurus luii

Goniurosaurus yingdeensis

Lichtenfelderi group:

Goniurosaurus hainanensis

Goniurosaurus lichtenfelderi

Kuroiwae group:

Goniurosaurus kuroiwae

Goniurosaurus orientalis

Goniurosaurus splendens

Goniurosaurus toyamai

Goniurosaurus yamashinae

Recently described species not assigned to a group:

Goniurosaurus liboensis

Goniurosaurus kadoorieorum

Goniurosaurus kwangsiensis

Goniurosaurus zhelongi

name *araneus* means "spider-like," referring to its spindly, long-limbed build. This species reaches a length of 7.5 inches (19 cm), making it one of the biggest species of cave gecko.

G. bawangliengensis is restricted to Hainan Island, a Chinese island off the country's southern coast. The availability of this gecko is severely limited because its natural range is believed to be entirely within the Bawangling National Nature Reserve. Its snout–vent length is just over 4 inches (10 cm). It has a stockier build than most other gonis.

G. catbaensis was first described as a distinct species in 2008. It is found in northeastern Vietnam in the Ong Bi Valley and the nearby Cat Ba Islands. Hobbyists refer to this species as the Cat Ba leopard gecko or Cat Ba cave gecko.

G. huuliensis is also found in northeastern Vietnam, including within the Huu Lien-Yen Thinh Nature Reserve. It may also occur in adjacent areas of China. It is believed to be the largest species in the genus, reaching a total length of just over 9 inches (23 cm).

G. luii lives in the Chinese provinces of Guangxi and Hainan as well as in adjacent areas of Vietnam. On Hainan, its range overlaps that of the Hainan cave gecko, *G. hainanensis*. Unfortunately, demand for this species resulted in overcollection, and there are now places within its range where it has been extirpated, including the type locality of Pingxiang in Guangxi. Hobbyists refer to *G. luii* as the Chinese leopard gecko or Chinese cave gecko. It is one of the largest of the gonis, reaching a length of about 7.5 inches (19 cm).

G. yingdeensis hails from the northern parts of Guangdong Province, China, and was discovered in 2010. It was initially found near Yingde, from where its name derives.

The Lichtenfelderi Group

Only two species belong to the Lichtenfelderi group: *Goniurosaurus hainanensis*, and *G. lichtenfelderi*. These two species inhabit forested islands off Vietnam and China and are both banded in yellow against a darker background.

As the name suggests, *G. hainanensis* is found on the island of Hainan from the foothills up to the forested mountains. It is known in the hobby as the Hainan leopard gecko and Hainan cave gecko. It reaches a length of almost 6.5 inches (16.5 cm). This is one of the more frequently seen gonis in the reptile trade because it is bred in greater numbers than most of the others, especially by European hobbyists.

Goniurosaurus lichtenfelderi.

G. lichtenfelderi is found on the Norway Islands off northeastern Vietnam. There is also an isolated population of this species on mainland Vietnam; it was once named *G. murphyi* but was determined to actually be *G. lichenfelderi* by Grismer (2000). It inhabits lowland forests and is typically found near limestone crevices, caves, and outcroppings (Grismer 2002).

The Kuroiwae Group

This group of geckos is found on various islands in the Ryukyu Archipelago of Japan. For that reason, this species in this group—*Goniurosaurus kuroiwae*, *G. orientalis*, *G. splendens*, *G. toyamai*, and *G. yamashinae*—are often called Japanese leopard geckos and Japanese cave geckos. Most of these species were once considered subspecies of *G. kuroiwae*, but because of their geographic isolation from each other and consistent physical differences, they are now considered full species. Japan considers all of these species as national monuments and protects them from collection. However, there is significant poaching of these lizards.

As a group, these are the smallest of the cave geckos. They average between 5.5 and 6.5 inches (14–16.5 cm). *G. yamashinae* has golden eyes, while the rest of the species have deep red eyes. All are darkly colored with more brightly colored bands and blotches.

G. kuroiwae is called the Okinawan leopard gecko, the Okinawan cave gecko, and Kuroiwa's leopard gecko. It is found on Okinawa and two other nearby islands, Sesoko and Kouri. *G. kuroiwae* has bands of bright pink against its chocolate-brown background color.

The natural range of *G. orientalis* is spread over several islands to the west of Okinawa: Kumejima, Tonakijima, Tokashikijima, Akajima, Iejima, and Iheyajima. There are some differences between the *G. orientalis* found on different islands, leading some herpetologists and breeders to believe that there are several species hidden under this name. Most *G. orientalis* have bright red-orange bands with white bands on their tails.

Goniurosaurus orientalis.

One of the Japanese cave geckos, (*Goniurosaurus splendens*).

G. splendens lives in limestone caves and crevices in the interior of Tokunoshima Island, the most northerly of the Ryukyu Islands. This species has bright pink bands on a very dark brown—almost black—background. This is the smallest of the gonis, with females reaching a maximum size of about 5.5 inches (14 cm).

G. toyamai is found only on Iheyajima, which is due north of Okinawa. Despite being listed as critically endangered, this species is present in the reptile trade in small numbers; these are likely illegally smuggled animals or the offspring of such. They are quite similar in appearance to *G. splendens* but have stockier bodies.

Kumejima Island is the only home to the cave gecko *G. yamashinae*.

G. yamashinae is found only on Kumejima Island and is considered endangered. It is the biggest species in this group, with some individuals reaching a little longer than 7 inches (18 cm). *G. yamashinae* hatches with white bands on a black background. As the gecko ages, the bands turn yellow.

CARE

Despite the many species of gonis and the huge area over which they are found, caring for these cave geckos is essentially the same across the group. They need cool and humid conditions, much like those required by cat geckos.

Most of the cave geckos found in the hobby are wild caught, but captive-bred individuals of some of the species are becoming more readily available. Herpetologists urge prospective keepers to seek out cave geckos bred in captivity because they are healthier and easier to keep. Buying captive-bred animals also prevents fanciers from unknowingly purchasing animals that were illegally poached from the wild. When bringing a cave gecko home, it is best to practice quarantine and use a simplified setup for the first six or eight weeks (see Chapter 3).

All cave geckos are shy and easily stressed, so house them singly and do not handle them more often than necessary. If you decide to house your cave geckos in groups, do not house males with other males.

Housing

A single cave gecko will do well in a 15-gallon (57-liter) aquarium or equivalent (24 x 12 x 12 inches [61 x 30 x 30 cm]). You can house cave geckos in sweater boxes, but they will climb if given space and an opportunity to do so. *G. araneus, G. catbaensis,* and G. *luii* are especially prone to climbing and will actively hunt in branches and on top of rocks.

A substrate that holds humidity, such as coconut bedding, reptile bark, soil, and sphagnum moss, is necessary, and you can top the substrate with leaf litter. Cave geckos adapt well to humid vivaria with soil, drainage, and live plants; see the section on cat geckos in this chapter for a discussion on constructing a live, humid vivarium.

Because of cave geckos' shy dispositions, provide plenty of hiding areas and cover. Cork bark tubes and manufactured caves work as hides, and you can glue rocks together to form caves and crevices much like the geckos would encounter in their natural habitats. Take care that the geckos cannot shift the rocks and be crushed. Always include more hiding places in the enclosure than there are geckos. Also provide at least one humidified hide box with moistened sphagnum or coconut husk so the geckos can retire to a moist shelter.

Heat and Humidity

Cave geckos inhabit cool microhabitats in their rainforest homes. In general, they do well with temperatures in the upper 70s (around 26°C) during the day, dropping down to the upper 60s (around 20°C) at night. However, there are some variations among the different species. The Kuroiwae group cannot tolerate temperatures above 82°F (28°C) for very long. G. *luii,* G. *araneus,* and G. *lichtenfelderi* can do well at temperatures in the low 80s (around 28°C), but they don't need temperatures that high to thrive.

Keep the vivarium's humidity at 80 percent or higher, which will usually require either nightly misting along with a humidity-retaining substrate or a humidifier or misting system.

Feeding

Gonis can be fed much like leopard geckos and other eublepharids (see Chapter 4). Gut-load all prey as appropriate for the species, and supplement cave geckos as directed for leopard geckos. Feed cave geckos roughly every other night, removing any uneaten prey in the morning, and provide them access to fresh water at all times.

BREEDING

The mysteries of breeding *Goniurosaurus* have been unraveling since around 2005. Although they are still not commonly bred by hobbyists, more captive-bred cave geckos are produced every year.

Adult males usually have easily seen hemipenal bulges. In most species of *Goniurosaurus*, the females are larger than the males.

Breeders have the most consistent success with cave geckos by providing a cooling period of about two months before breeding. Temperatures during the cool period can go as low as 55°F (13°C) at night, although the temperature likely doesn't need to go below 60°F (16°C).

During the warmer period, the geckos will breed. If housing your gonis singly, move a male to a female's enclosure; she will lay eggs approximately thirty days after mating. Provide a laying box with moistened perlite or vermiculite in which the female can nest. Even with a nesting box, however, she is likely to lay eggs elsewhere in the cage. The best way to get a female to lay in a nesting box is to make sure it is the warmest, most humid place in her enclosure, as these are the criteria by which females choose their laying sites. Females may lay four to six clutches a year.

Incubate the eggs in moist conditions like those required for adults. A temperature range of 75–79°F (24–26°C) will work for most species. *G. orientalis* eggs likely need cooler temperatures, given the natural habitat of the species. A range of 72–75°F (22–24°C) may be best for this species.

Incubation time varies by species, temperature, and other factors. In general, expect the eggs to hatch in fifty-five to eighty-five days. Set up the hatchlings like adults, but scale the enclosures and furnishings down for their smaller size. As long as the hatchlings are all close to the same size, you can house them together for the first few months.

Hatchlings normally shed within twenty-four hours of hatching and will eat soon after they shed. Feed them small insects and invertebrates, such as pinhead crickets, flightless fruit flies, baby roaches, isopods, and hatchling silkworms.

> ### Did You Know?
> Hatchling cave geckos are vulnerable to dehydration, so pay careful attention to the humidity in their enclosures.

REFERENCES

Allen, R. 1987. "Captive Care and Breeding of the Leopard Gecko, *Eublepharis macularius.*" *Reptiles: Proceedings of the 1986 U.K. Herpetological Societies' Symposium on Captive Breeding* 27–30.

Anderson, A., and C. Oldham. 1986. "Captive Husbandry and Propagation of the African Fat-Tail Gecko, *Hemitheconyx caudicinctus.*" *Proceedings of the 10th International Herpetological Symposium on Captive Propagation and Husbandry* 75–85.

Autum, K., and D. F. De Nardo. 1995. "Thermoregulation and Growth Rates in Leopard Geckos." *Journal of Herpetology* 29:157–62.

Bull, J. J. 1980. "Sex Determination in Reptiles." *The Quarterly Review of Biology* 55: 2–21.

———. 1987. "Temperature-Dependent Sex Determination in Reptiles: Validity of Sex Diagnosis in Hatchling Lizards." *Canadian Journal of Zoology* 65:1421–24.

DiPrima, A. M., B. E. Viets, and C. F. Williams. 1997. "The Effects of Sex, Incubation Temperature, and Heritability on Pigmentation in the Leopard Gecko, *Eublepharis macularius.*" *Proceedings of the 77th Annual Meeting of the American Society of Ichthyologists and Herpetologists.*

Gamble, T. 1997. *A Leopard Gecko Bibliography.* Self-published.

Grismer, L. I. 1988. "Phylogeny, Taxonomy, Classification, and Biogeography of Eublepharid Geckos." In *Phylogenetic Relationships of the Lizard Families, edited by R. Estes and G. Pregill, 369-469.* Stanford, CA: Stanford University Press.

———. 1997. *"Eublepharid Geckos: Living Relics of Gekkotan Evolution." Fauna* 1:1.

Gutzke, W. H. N., and D. Crews. 1988. "Embryonic Temperature Determines Adult Sexuality in a Reptile." *Nature* 332:832–34.

Heidemann, R. L., and B. E. Viets. 1995. "The Effects of Incubation Temperature on Sex and Growth in the Gecko, *Hemitheconyx caudicinctus.*" *Proceedings of the 75th Annual Meeting of the American Society of Ichthyologists and Herpetologists.*

———. 1996. "The Effect of Male Body Size on Dominance and Mate Acquisition in the Gecko, *Hemitheconyx caudicinctus.*" *Proceedings of the 39th Annual Meeting of the Society for the Study of Amphibians and Reptiles.*

Lui, W. 1996. "Captive Husbandry and Breeding of the Malaysian Cat Gecko, *Aeluroscalabotes felinus." International Reptilian* 4:3.

Nunan, J. 1987. "Prevention of Dehydration and Calcium Depletion in Deserticolous Geckos." in *Captive Propagation and Husbandry of Reptiles and Amphibians, 4:43–47.* Sacramento: Northern California Herpetological Society.

Slavens, F., and K. Slavens. 1997. *Reptiles and Amphibians in Captivity: Breeding, Longevity and Inventory.* Seattle, WA: Slaveware.

Thorogood, J., and I. W. Whimster. 1979. "The Maintenance and Breeding of the Leopard Gecko, *Eublepharis macularius*, As a Laboratory Animal." *International Zoo Yearbook* 19:74–78.

Tousignant, A., B. Viets, D. Flores, and D. Crews. 1995. "Ontogenetic and Social Factors Affect the Endocrinology and Timing of Reproduction in the Female Leopard Gecko, *Eublepharis macularius.*" *Hormones and Behavior* 29:141–53.

Viets, B. E., M. A. Ewert, L. G. Talent, and C. E. Nelson. 1994. "Sex-Determining Mechanisms in Squamate Reptiles." *The Journal of Experimental Zoology* 270:45–56.

Viets, B. E., A. Tousignant, M. A. Ewert, C. E. Nelson, and D. Crews. 1993. "Temperature-Dependent Sex Determination in the Leopard Gecko, *Eublepharis macularius.*" *The Journal of Experimental Zoology* 265:679–83.

Wagner, E. 1974. "Breeding of the Leopard Gecko, *Eublepharis macularius*, at the Seattle Zoo." *International Zoo Yearbook* 14:84–86.

Wise, S. 1994. "An Analysis of Behavioral Interactions in the Leopard Gecko, *Eublepharis macularius.*" *Proceedings of the 104th Annual Meeting of the Nebraska Academy of Sciences.*

Yaverkin, Y. I., and N. L. Orlov. 1998. "Captive Breeding of Cat Geckos." *Dactylus* 3:3, 87–89.

INDEX

Note: Page numbers in *italics* indicate captions. Page ranges in parentheses indicate non-contiguous references within the range.

PHOTO CREDITS

ACKNOWLEDGMENTS

My heartfelt thanks go out to my collaborators on these various projects: David Crews, Adam DiPrima, Michael Ewert, Deborah Flores, Richard Heidemann, Craig Nelson, Larry Talent, Alan Tousignant, Rick Williams, and Steve Wise. Larry and Rich deserve special mention as good friends and fellow lizard lovers. Larry is the authority on lizard keeping in academe, and Rich has been my right-hand man for years.

Because of the rapid changes in leopard gecko herpetoculture, it became clear that to write an up-to-date book on the subject I needed to seek the help and advice of other specialists. The quality of information gathered in this book would have not been possible without the coauthors: my good friend Roger Klingenberg, DVM, who has joined me on several writing ventures; Ron Tremper, a pioneer in the domestication of leopard geckos who developed several of the popular designer morphs; and Brian Viets, PhD, an expert on the effects of temperature on sex determination and skin pigmentation in leopard geckos. In addition to the chapters each wrote, all three contributed to information throughout the book.

Many other specialist breeders, in an admirable spirit of cooperation and support, provided invaluable help, information, and photos. Special thanks to Bill Brant, David Nieves, Tim Rainwater, David Northcott, Bill Love, Richard Bartlett, Mark Leshock, Tom Weidner, and Sean McKeown.

ABOUT THE AUTHORS

Philippe de Vosjoli is the highly acclaimed author of the best-selling Herpetocultural Library Series of reptile-care books. His work in the field of herpetoculture has been recognized nationally and internationally for establishing high standards for amphibian and reptile care. His books, articles, and other writings have been praised and recommended by numerous herpetological societies, veterinarians, and other experts in the field. De Vosjoli is also the cofounder and former president of the American Federation of Herpetoculturists, and he received the Josef Laszlo Memorial Award for excellence in herpetoculture and his contributions to the advancement of the field.

Thomas Mazorlig earned his bachelor's degree in biology from Cornell University and has edited reptile and amphibian books and magazines since 1999, most recently serving as editor-in-chief of *Pet Age* magazine. He has written numerous articles and several books on the care and breeding of reptiles and amphibians and has kept and bred king, corn, and pine snakes; bearded dragons; and several species of chameleons. Mazorlig currently keeps several tarantulas and snakes and has recently become a reef-tank hobbyist.

Roger Klingenberg, DVM, founded Sheep Draw Veterinary Hospital in Greeley, Colorado, in 1985, seven years after graduating from Colorado State's veterinary program. In addition to caring for his patients, Dr. Klingenberg keeps his own snakes, lizards, turtles, tortoises, and even insects. He breeds rare reptiles and is a respected expert on exotic-pet care, specializing in medicine and surgery in exotics, orthopedic surgery (especially knees) in dogs and cats, laser surgery, and preventative healthcare; he is a prolific author and speaker on these and other veterinary topics.

Ron Tremper is an expert in leopard gecko breeding and care and is recognized worldwide as a herpetoculture pioneer and a leading authority on leopard geckos. During his decades of experience, Tremper has held tenure as curator of reptiles at the Fresno Zoo in Fresno, California; received breeding awards from the American Zoo Association; and served as reptile expert for Tetrafauna. At the time of publication, Tremper was celebrating thirty-nine generations of unbroken leopard gecko bloodlines that are responsible for many of the most popular color, size, and pattern morphs in the species.

Brian Viets, PhD, is a reptile specialist who has been associated with prestigious academic institutions, including Indiana University and Nebraska Wesleyan University, during his career. Dr. Viets has contributed his expertise to numerous published research papers and reptile books. Most notably, he has conducted and published extensive research on temperature-dependent sex determination in the leopard gecko as well as sex-determining mechanisms in other reptiles.